# Your • Money • Ratios

# Your • Money • Ratios

*8 Simple Tools for*
*Financial Security at Every Stage of Life*

## Charles Farrell, J.D., LL.M.

AVERY

*a member of Penguin Group (USA) Inc.*

NEW YORK

Published by the Penguin Group

Penguin Group (USA) Inc., 375 Hudson Street, New York, New York 10014, USA • Penguin Group (Canada), 90 Eglinton Avenue East, Suite 700, Toronto, Ontario M4P 2Y3, Canada (a division of Pearson Penguin Canada Inc.) • Penguin Books Ltd, 80 Strand, London WC2R 0RL, England • Penguin Ireland, 25 St Stephen's Green, Dublin 2, Ireland (a division of Penguin Books Ltd) • Penguin Group (Australia), 250 Camberwell Road, Camberwell, Victoria 3124, Australia (a division of Pearson Australia Group Pty Ltd) • Penguin Books India Pvt Ltd, 11 Community Centre, Panchsheel Park, New Delhi–110 017, India • Penguin Group (NZ), 67 Apollo Drive, Rosedale, North Shore 0632, New Zealand (a division of Pearson New Zealand Ltd) • Penguin Books (South Africa) (Pty) Ltd, 24 Sturdee Avenue, Rosebank, Johannesburg 2196, South Africa

Penguin Books Ltd, Registered Offices: 80 Strand, London WC2R 0RL, England

First paperback edition 2010

Most Avery books are available at special quantity discounts for bulk purchase for sales promotions, premiums, fund-raising, and educational needs. Special books or book excerpts also can be created to fit specific needs. For details, write Penguin Group (USA) Inc. Special Markets, 375 Hudson Street, New York, NY 10014.

Library of Congress Cataloging-in-Publication Data

Farrell, Charles, J. D.
Your money ratios : 8 simple tools for financial security at every stage of life / Charles Farrell.
p.      cm.
Includes index.
ISBN 978-1-58333-416-4
1. Retirement income.    2. Finance, Personal.    3. Financial security.    I. Title.
HG179.F3623    2010                          2010028804
332.024—dc22

Printed in the United States of America
1   3   5   7   9   10   8   6   4   2

*Book design by Jennifer Ann Daddio/Bookmark Design & Media Inc.*

# CONTENTS

Introduction | A Simple, New Perspective  *1*

1 | The Capital to Income Ratio  *15*

2 | The Savings Ratio  *28*

3 | Social Security  *48*

4 | Where to Save Your Money  *59*

5 | The Debt Ratios  *75*

6 | The Investment Ratio  *112*

7 | Stocks and Bonds 101  *138*

8 | Ignoring Wall Street  *159*

9 | The Disability Insurance Ratio  *167*

10 | The Life Insurance Ratio     *178*

11 | The Long-Term Care
      Insurance Ratio     *188*

12 | Health Insurance     *207*

13 | Getting Professional Help     *221*

14 | Pulling It All Together     *235*


*Appendix* | *Special Situations*     *239*

*Acknowledgments*     *247*

*Index*     *249*

# Your • Money • Ratios

# A Simple, New Perspective

What does the word "retirement" mean to you? If your first thoughts were of complicated financial statements and watching the stock market with anxiety, you're not alone. Many Americans are intimidated by the idea of building a financial foundation for a secure, enjoyable retirement. While retiring early to a life of leisure is perhaps the true American Dream, it's beginning to feel more remote than ever: according to the Employee Benefit Research Institute's 2009 Retirement Confidence Survey, only 13% of workers are very confident about saving enough money for a comfortable retirement, down from 18% in 2008 and 27% in 2007. As the economy gets shakier, our confidence in our ability to plan for retirement has done the same, but it doesn't have to be that way.

It's possible to lead a healthy financial life today and set yourself on the path to a secure retirement. The secret is having a perspective on your money that is both simple and productive, allowing you to gain a clear understanding of your most critical financial decisions and take action that delivers consistent, positive results. You don't have to become an investment expert to manage your financial life wisely; that's why people like me are in business. You just need fresh tools, and that's what makes *Your Money Ratios* unique.

## The Magic of Ratios

This book presents a series of elegant, simple formulas for managing the most important aspects of your personal finances, all with the goal of helping you make steady progress toward a secure retirement while living more securely and sensibly today and being buttressed against disability, disease, tragedy, or downturns in the future. The key is the simple ratio. Don't lapse into a high school math class coma; this is easy to grasp. A ratio is nothing more than the relation between two numbers expressed like this: 2:1.

The beauty of *Your Money Ratios* is that it turns all those mind-numbing financial calculations into simple ratios based on your age and household income. That's the fresh tool. Nothing more complicated than that. If you know how old you are and how much you make, you can master your retirement planning. You do know how old you are and how much you make, right?

If you would like to lead a healthy financial life and set yourself on the path to a secure retirement, then this is the book for you. While there are many books about personal finance and retirement, this book is unique. It provides a simple and clear framework for understanding what you need to do today to prepare yourself for a more secure future.

*Your Money Ratios* will help you understand how to manage the four core areas of personal finance:

1. Savings
2. Debt
3. Investments
4. Insurance

To lead a healthy financial life and position yourself for a secure retirement, you must manage these four areas in concert. In theory, this is not difficult to do if you understand the methods and reasons behind it. The trouble is that money is an emotional issue. Even experienced financial professionals become caught up in the emotional ups and downs of the real estate market or the stock market. Witness the financial crisis of 2008 and 2009. A great deal of that turmoil came about because even the Wall Street whizzes allowed their desire for profit to overcome their good sense and convince them that somehow, the real estate market would keep appreciating forever. Well, 100 years of financial data have showed us that nothing appreciates forever, but emotions blinded many to this truth, and the result was the worst financial meltdown since the Great Depression—exacerbated by emotion as people quit spending out of fear and pulled their money out of the falling stock market out of blind panic.

The formulas you will learn in this book are designed to help you take the emotion out of your retirement savings as much as possible. By following them steadily and consistently over the years, you will avoid making bad decisions based on "irrational exuberance," or fear. For example, when the stock market is up, many people increase the size of their investments, forgetting that what goes up must come down. And when the market plummets as it did in late 2008, people who are making their decisions based on emotions tend to get out, believing they can "time the market" and get back in just as stocks are about to rise. The truth is, no one can time the market. The only thing you do by pulling your money out of a down market is increase the odds that you will make another bad decision on when to get back in, one that could cost you tens of thousands of dollars or more.

*Your Money Ratios* takes emotion out of saving for retirement. You simply follow the numbers consistently, year after year, and do your best to ignore what everyone else is doing or where the market goes. Over time, if you invest and make your financial decisions this way, you are likely to reach your goals. A century of financial and economic facts bear this out, time and time again. When it comes to your money and your future, you want to be Mr. Spock, not James T. Kirk.

## The Five Questions

If you are like most people, you find it difficult to answer the following questions:

1. How much should I be saving each year?
2. How much should I have saved at my age?
3. How much debt should I carry?
4. How do I invest my savings?
5. What insurance do I need?

Even with the substantial amount of information available on these subjects, most people are completely confused about how to manage a modern financial life and prepare for a secure retirement. There are two primary reasons for this. First, financial services companies have a vested interest in marketing their products to us. Second, today's financial markets and suites of investment products are so complex that rocket scientists and neurosurgeons are left saying, "Huh?" Yet these are the most important questions in your entire financial life.

At this point you may be holding up your hands and saying, "Whoa, Charlie, I don't know this! This is why I hire a financial advisor!" That's exactly my point. You need to answer these questions in order for your financial advisor to do his or her job well. But even with the substantial amount of financial information available on these subjects, people are confused about how to manage a modern financial life and prepare for a secure retirement. There's a lot of noise and very little signal. Yet your financial future depends on knowing the answers.

*Your Money Ratios* provides the answers. It takes all the complex questions of today's finances and reduces them to a simple set of eight financial ratios. The ratios are based on your household income (pretax) and age. Thus, the ratios can be used by anyone at any age to help determine how much you should be saving, how much you should have saved at your age, how much debt you can carry, how to invest your savings, and what type of insurance you need at each stage of life.

*Your Money Ratios* provides you with an incredibly simple and practical tool for managing the most important aspects of your financial life. The ratios cover the time frame from ages 25 to 65, and help you make the important decisions in the four core areas of finance throughout your adult working years. This isn't about getting rich; it's about developing a long-term perspective for prudently managing your finances and steadily building assets for retirement. It is based on sound financial principles that have stood the test of time, not gimmicks.

## Appropriate for Any Age

The ratios are derived from the concept of financial ratios that major corporations and prudent investors have used for decades to make profitable business decisions. I have taken that basic concept and adapted it to personal finance. The reason financial ratios work so well is because they provide clarity of purpose and serve as an excellent tool for financial decision making. If a decision doesn't match up with the numbers dictated by prudent ratios, then it is not the right decision and you shouldn't make it.

One of the biggest problems with personal finance (aside from runaway emotion) is that we don't apply the same type of financial discipline as we do in business. That is why many businesses are highly profitable and many households are struggling. If you are reading this introduction, then I expect that you are interested in getting your finances in better shape. It is a great feeling once you gain control over your finances and begin to build financial independence.

If you follow the guidelines in *Your Money Ratios*, you should put yourself in a position to retire in your mid 60s on about 80% of the income you were earning prior to retirement. At the same time, you will be living a healthy financial life today. Both of these objectives are balanced within *Your Money Ratios*.

In a nutshell, the book will help you determine:

1. How much total savings you should have accumulated at your age.
2. How much you should be saving each year.
3. What tax and investment vehicles you should use to maximize your savings.
4. How much mortgage and education debt you should be carrying at your age.
5. How to manage your investments for prudent growth and principal protection.
6. How to purchase the disability, life, health, and long-term care insurance necessary to protect your income and assets.

If you are in your 20s or 30s, *Your Money Ratios* will tell you how to get started and what you need to do over the next 35 years to stay on track. If you are lucky enough to read this book when you are young, you will have a clear vision for where you need to go throughout your working career. By setting yourself on the right path, you won't have to work so hard later in life to meet your goals.

If you are in your 40s, you can benchmark your own financial circumstances against the ratios and see how you are doing with respect to your savings, debt, investments, and insurance. You have plenty of time to make adjustments if necessary and plot out your path to retirement.

If you are in your 50s, the formula will provide you with a realistic assessment of your ability to retire. It will help you make the important decisions about how to allocate your financial resources over the next 10 to 15 years, and how to put on the final push for retirement.

## What You Will Find in This Book

*Your Money Ratios* is built around four major sections, one for each of the four core areas of personal finance: savings, debt, investments, and insurance. Within each section, I explain the fundamental theory behind how to manage that particular area of personal finance. It is important to have a basic understanding of the theory because it puts *Your Money Ratios* in its proper perspective. I then set forth the financial ratios that apply to that particular area of personal finance. Woven among these four core sections is additional supporting material that will help you develop the fresh perspective you'll need to properly put the ratios into action.

The heart of this book is a matrix that includes the eight ratios I have developed during my career as an attorney specializing in taxation and later as a financial advisor. In the first chapter, I introduce the Capital to Income Ratio, which tells you how much capital (savings) you should have accumulated at your age to stay on track for retirement. I then move to the Savings Ratio in the next chapter and fill out the ratio matrix as we continue through the book. Each section builds on the prior material, and the matrix table allows you to easily follow the ratios as they build on each other. By the end of the book, you will find all of the ratios summarized in one easy-to-use table. Just consult the matrix and know your age to benchmark your current finances and see the path going forward.

In the savings chapter, I will help you understand how much of your income you need to be saving each year so that you can reach your Capital to Income Ratio each year. You can use these ratios to benchmark the progress you are making toward a secure retirement. In this chapter, I will also get into detail about the key savings accounts—IRAs, 401(k)s, and others—where you should be putting your money.

In the debt section, I will address mortgage debt first because it is the largest debt you're likely to carry. While owning a home is a good goal, excessive mortgage debt will consume so much of your monthly budget that you'll have no money available for your savings goals. The Mortgage to Income Ratio is designed to keep housing debt in proper proportion to your income, and provide you with enough room in the budget to hit your savings goals.

Education debt comes next because not only is it usually substantial, but it's directly related to your earning potential. This material applies to anyone thinking of taking on debt to go to school and to parents thinking about taking on debt to help their kids finance college.

In the investment section, I'll teach you how to build a globally diversified and well-balanced investment portfolio, even in these unnerving and volatile times. That sounds like a tall order, but it is much easier than you think if you focus on the fundamentals and quit wasting your time watching the financial markets every day. My investment ratios will provide you with guidance on how to construct your investment portfolio at each age to help you achieve a more consistent and realistic rate of return.

In the insurance section, I will help you understand the sole purpose of insurance: to protect your income and assets. At various ages you will need different types of insurance because you are facing different types of financial risks. In this chapter, you will find insurance ratios for life, disability, and long-term care insurance, the three primary forms of personal insurance that are critical to retirement planning. I'll also spend time talking about health insurance, because health-care costs will be one of the biggest liabilities we all will face. It helps to understand the potential costs and benefits of insurance so that you can take the proper steps throughout your working career to prepare yourself for those expenses.

## Wise Decisions, Realistic Assumptions

Near the end of the book, I spend a chapter talking about getting help with your personal financial decisions. Although you will have a tremendous amount of knowledge about what to do by the time you finish the book, today's financial landscape remains dizzyingly complex. This book is not a substitute for individual advice; no book can be. In the "Getting Professional Help" chapter, I share my best advice for making a smart decision in choosing a financial profes-sional to assist you with planning to reach your long-term goals. Hint: it's not the advisor who promises you the glitzy return. In sum-mary, *Your Money Ratios* provides you with an incredibly practical, simple, and effective tool for managing your finances. The logic of the formula will transform how you think about and live your finan-cial life.

In developing financial ratios or doing financial projections, pro-fessionals need to make certain assumptions about the growth of the economy, investments, interest rates, wage growth, housing costs, in-flation, and many other items. Fortunately, we have a vast repository of exhaustively analyzed data to help us do just this. The assumptions used to develop *Your Money Ratios* are based on data about the econ-omy and financial and employment markets collected over the last 100 years, which is generally regarded as the period of modern finance.

History provides valuable insight into what we may experience in the future, but it is by no means a predictor of future events. That's why I attempt to be conservative with my assumptions.

Long-term financial returns tend to fluctuate within a range, and I generally use the long-term averages and ignore the extreme moves in shorter cycles. This will help you develop additional discipline and increases the likelihood that the ratios will deliver the results you desire.

I bring this up because there will be sections of the book where I will use assumptions that deviate from your recent experience in the financial, real estate, debt, or employment markets. There is a sound reason for this: during any short-term period, markets can vary significantly, as anyone paying attention to the real estate market or stock prices in 2008 and 2009 can attest. It is dangerous to your future to put too much emphasis on short-term numbers. Dramatic highs and lows rarely last. Reversion to the long-term mean is the rule of thumb in the financial markets, no matter what the trend watchers and financial magazines say.

For instance, periods of high investment returns are often followed by periods of low investment returns; and conversely, periods of low returns are often followed by periods of high returns. When you average them all out, you get a much better sense of the long-term trends, which is closer to what you are likely to experience over both your working career and years in retirement. If you focus on the short term, you may end up making either overly optimistic or overly pessimistic assumptions. I will spend more time discussing various assumptions as we move through the book, but it is important to keep in mind the general rule that using long-term trend numbers is the most prudent method of planning.

## The Unifying Theory of Personal Finance

In all areas of study, it is important to understand the fundamental theories of that field. For instance, if you are a physicist, you will want to understand the fundamental law of gravity. That under-standing will help shape your approach to other problems in phys-ics. If you don't, you might spend a lot of time designing a rocket that can't get off the ground.

In personal finance, there is a fundamental theory that should link all of your decisions. This theory serves as the foundation for the development of *Your Money Ratios*, and I call it the Unifying Theory of Personal Finance. It is this:

> All decisions you make should help move you
> from being a laborer to being a capitalist.

I will repeat it again because it is so important: *All decisions you make should help move you from being a laborer to being a capitalist.* That sounds good, but what does it mean? As a laborer, you are paid a wage for your services. It does not matter if you are a police officer, factory worker, doctor, lawyer, scientist, clerk, landscaper, or base-ball player. You are paid a wage for doing some form of work. You are exchanging work for money, which means you must labor for your money, and are thus a laborer.

Don't get sidetracked by the political connotations associated with the words "laborer" and "capitalist." Laborer refers to the pro-cess of working to generate income, not a certain type of worker. All of us are laborers. As a capitalist, you are paid not for the *value of your labor*, but *for the use of your money*. This payment can come in the form of interest, dividends, or price appreciation, but in one way or another, you are being paid to allow others to use your money. This is the essence of investing, and thus being a capitalist. If you hope to retire someday, you will need to become a capitalist—someone who generates income from their capital.

This is how labor and capital are related. You must start out as a laborer to generate income. You then save a portion of that income every year. Those savings become your investment capital. As your capital builds, the payment for the use of your money grows. Once your capital is large enough, the payment for the use of your money will replace your wages, and you can retire.

If you hope to retire someday, it is very important for you to understand the transformation you must eventually make with your personal finances. This long-term goal of moving from laborer to capitalist will guide the basic financial decisions you make throughout your working career. *Your Money Ratios* lays out the path you must travel to move from laborer to capitalist. This is generally a 40-year process that starts in your mid 20s and ends sometime in your mid 60s. It usually takes each of us that long to build up enough capital such that the income from that capital can replace our wages.

## The Unifying Question

To make that journey from laborer to capitalist, you must effectively manage the core issues of personal finance: deciding how much to save each year, how much capital you should have accumulated at each age, how much debt to carry, how to prudently invest your capital, and how to purchase insurance to protect your capital. The ratios provide you with guidance in each of these areas at every stage of life. And because our underlying theory is about moving from being a laborer to being a capitalist, at the start of every section I will ask what I call the Unifying Question:

> Will this financial decision help move me from being a laborer to being a capitalist?

Keeping that basic transformation in mind will clarify the purpose of all your important financial decisions. If it doesn't help you make that transformation, then it is probably the wrong decision. If it does help, then you are on the right track. It is important to note that the question contains the word "help." The process of moving from laborer to capitalist is a culmination of many good decisions over a three- to four-decade time frame. Some decisions will help more than others, but when you consistently make good decisions, you will be making steady progress.

# 1

# The Capital to Income Ratio

The concept of moving from laborer to capitalist sounds like a nice theory, but what you probably want to know most of all about retirement is this: "How much savings (capital) will I need to retire?" A good estimate is that you will need to accumulate capital worth about 12 times your income. If you have capital worth about 12 times your gross annual income at age 65, this should put you in a position to live on about 80% of your preretirement income. I will explain how this works, later in the chapter.

This is the transformation from laborer to capitalist. You start out with zero capital when you are young, save a portion of your income each year, and ultimately try to accumulate capital worth 12 times your pay. To help you track and benchmark the accumulation of your capital, I have developed the Capital to Income Ratio, or CIR. The CIR tells you how much capital you should have accumulated at various points between ages 25 and 65 so that you stay on track to reach 12 times pay at retirement. This time frame covers the general working years for most people, and lets you know if you are on track at a particular time. The CIR is the most important ratio in

*Your Money Ratios* because it provides the framework for your transition from laborer to capitalist. All of the other ratios are designed to help you meet your CIR.

## Figuring Your CIR

To begin, look up your age and the corresponding Capital to Income Ratio figure in the chart below. Then multiply your household income by the Capital to Income Ratio. This tells you how much capital you should have accumulated at your age. If you are adequately saving (we'll talk about how much you should be saving in the "Savings Ratio" chapter), you should be hitting these ratios along the way. Since your goal is to accumulate capital worth at least 12 times your income, this ratio lays out your path from ages 25 to 65. All you need to do is keep driving your Capital to Income Ratio up so you are hitting each benchmark as you progress toward retirement. You do that by consistently saving each month, as well as properly managing your debt, investments, and insurance, which we will cover later.

Example: Let's assume you are 40 and have a household income of $100,000. The Capital to Income Ratio at age 40 is 2.4. This means you should have 2.4 times your income in savings, or $240,000 saved. Now add up what is in your 401(k), IRAs, savings, and investment accounts and compare it to that figure. This will tell you if you are ahead or behind in your goals. By using the ratios, you can quickly benchmark your progress and stay on track for retirement. If you are not on track, you can make adjustments and get back on track in a few years.

## CAPITAL TO INCOME RATIO

| Your age | Capital to Income Ratio (the multiple of your annual income you should have accumulated) |
|---|---|
| 25 | 0.1 |
| 30 | 0.6 |
| 35 | 1.4 |
| 40 | 2.4 |
| 45 | 3.7 |
| 50 | 5.2 |
| 55 | 7.1 |
| 60 | 9.4 |
| 65 | 12.0 |

For most people, the income component of the CIR will be easy to calculate. If you are paid a stable salary each year, you simply use your total household income for purposes of the CIR. But some people have a more volatile income stream. It might rise and fall as the result of a year-end bonus; or it is volatile because they are in sales or run their own business. In these cases, you want to use your "core" annual income for purposes of the CIR calculation. To calculate your core annual income, take a simple average of your pay for the last four years. This average will help smooth out the ups and downs, and give you a better sense of the average income you are living on each year.

The Capital to Income Ratio begins at age 25, when a good number of people start to enter the workforce. But I recognize that because of education requirements, such as graduate school, many people do not start their careers until their mid- to late 20s. So, between 25 and

30, it may be difficult for many people to begin accumulating much savings. This is also the time when people are paying back student loans, getting married, having kids, and trying to buy a house. Consequently, I don't expect that many people will be in a position to build much capital during their 20s. If you can accumulate capital equal to a little more than half of your salary, you will be doing pretty well. This is a modest amount, but a great start.

For the purposes of the CIR, capital means:

- The savings in your 401(k) plan, IRAs, annuities, and CDs
- The cash value of your life insurance
- The amount in your checking and savings accounts
- Equity in commercial real estate
- The fair market value of any business interests.

Capital does not include the equity in your home. Remember, being a capitalist is about being paid by others for the use of your money or assets. The house you live in does not generate income. If it were a rental or commercial property and you were allowing this asset to be used by others, you could expect some return. The real return you get from your own home is the rent-free use of the property once you pay off the mortgage. This will be very helpful to you in retirement, but the equity is generally unavailable as an income-producing asset because you are living there.

## Bob and Danielle

Let's take a hypothetical couple and see how they would use the Capital to Income Ratio. Bob and Danielle are both 45 years old and together they have a household income of $100,000. They have $170,000 in Bob's 401(k), $150,000 in Danielle's 401(k), and $50,000 in a brokerage account. Thus, they have a total of $370,000 in retirement savings.

According to the chart, at age 45, the CIR should be 3.7. Therefore, this family should have $370,000 of savings for retirement ($100,000 income × 3.7). In this example, Bob and Danielle are right on track. Over the next 20 years, as long as they keep on saving as they have been, their Capital to Income Ratio should steadily progress from 3.7 to 12. At that point, they could consider retiring. If they decided they wanted to retire early, they could save more and accelerate the process, but what makes the CIR important is that it sets your *minimum goal.* You know that as long as you are on target with this ratio, you should be able to retire at 65 on 80% of your income.

Now, if you benchmark your finances and determine you are ahead of the ratios, don't stop saving. There are many things that could throw you off course later in life. Continue to add consistently to your personal capital. The higher your CIR, the better. Alternatively, if you run your numbers and you are behind, don't worry, there are a couple of different paths you can take to retirement security, which I discuss later in this chapter.

## The 80% Solution

One question financial advisors often hear is:

"How can I live on 80% of my income in retirement?"

In short, you probably can. The reason 80% works is because your expense structure and tax situation changes significantly once you are in retirement. While you were working, you were saving a portion of your pay each year for retirement. Let's assume that was at least 12% of your pay, so in essence you were only living off 88% of your income. Plus, you were paying FICA (Social Security) taxes as an employee, which is another 7.65% of pay on the first $106,800 you earn in 2010 (this amount is indexed for inflation each year).

You also probably had a mortgage, which these days might be at least another 20% of pay. Consequently, while working you were probably only living on about 60% of your actual income.

## WHAT YOU REALLY LIVE ON

| Preretirement Take-home Pay | |
|---|---|
| Total Pay | 100% |
| Less Savings | 12% |
| Less FICA Taxes | 7.65% |
| Less Mortgage | 20% |
| **What You're Living On** | **60%** |

When you retire, you won't have to save anymore, you won't have a mortgage, and you won't pay FICA taxes. If you follow the advice I'm going to give you, you'll have virtually no debt of any kind. Thus, 80% of your total preretirement income should actually represent an *increase* in spendable income compared to your working days. You'll have more money in your hands to use as you please. Of course, you'll have some expenses that are higher, such as health insurance, and you'll still have some taxes to pay, but on balance, you should come out ahead.

## The 5% Rule

The second question advisors often hear is:

"How do I produce 80% of my income in retirement?"

Once you retire, we need to make some assumptions about how much of your money you can safely withdraw from your retirement savings each year. As I've said, we have a huge amount of data on the financial markets, going back over 100 years, and a good estimate is that you can withdraw about 5% of your savings each year. Here is how it works: if you were making $100,000 in annual income and are 65 years old, and you are on track with your CIR, you will have $1,200,000 of capital or savings (12 × $100,000).

In retirement, you should be able to withdraw about 5% of these funds every year for spending. Your investments will often be earning more than 5%, but because of inflation and the volatility associated with the financial markets, it's unwise to take out everything you earn each year. Therefore, the percentage of your money that you take out for spending needs to be smaller than the long-term annual return that you are earning. At a 5% distribution, you would have about $60,000 of income from your investments ($1,200,000 × 5% = $60,000). But didn't I say you would be living off 80% of your income, which would be $80,000? Where does the other $20,000 come from? *Social Security.*

Most people will qualify for a Social Security benefit. A lot of people ask me, "Can I depend on Social Security to be there when I retire?" In a word, yes. You can be reasonably confident that your Social Security benefit will be there. The Social Security program is funded one half by you and one half by your employer. In 2010, you each contribute 6.2% of the first $106,800 of your salary into the program every year. This is part of the FICA tax that is deducted from your paycheck every month. Regardless of how the program is restructured, there is a huge amount of your money going into Social Security for your retirement, and I think it is fair to assume that you will have a Social Security benefit.

In my ratios, I have discounted the future Social Security benefit to address the likelihood that there may be some reductions in benefits (but not an elimination of benefits). Thus, my conservative estimate is that Social Security payments will represent about 20% of most people's postretirement income. So if you earn $100,000 now, and get $60,000 from retirement savings, $20,000 from Social Security puts your total retirement income at $80,000, or 80% of your $100,000 salary. I'll talk more about Social Security and the many misconceptions about it in Chapter 3.

## How Not to Run Out of Money in Retirement

One thing investors often forget to account for in retirement is inflation. Inflation is the main reason we have to start with a lower initial distribution rate because the distributions need to grow to help maintain your lifestyle. This 5% distribution rate is designed to provide you with a reasonable probability of not running out of money during retirement. Even when you retire, inflation doesn't stop. Unless the economy is in a severe decline like we saw in 2009, the cost of things will continue to rise. So your 5% is a base, and you're going to increase the amount you take out each coming year to account for inflation.

The 5% rule is designed to give you some "spread" or cushion, so that even if you have to withdraw extra money to maintain your purchasing power, you're still earning a higher percentage than what you withdraw. The extra earnings go to help build your capital reserves and support higher total dollar distributions later.

Example: Assume you retire with $1,000,000 and begin to take your initial 5%, or $50,000, distribution. If inflation runs at 3.0%, then next year you would increase your $50,000 by 3%, for a total of $51,500. This additional $1,500 would allow you to buy the same amount of goods and services next year as you did this year. If inflation runs at 3.0% for 25 years, your initial $50,000 distribution will need to grow to $104,688 for you to maintain your purchasing power at the end of year 25—a 10% distribution of your $1,000,000 original account value.

Because your distributions must grow in retirement to keep up with the rising cost of energy, food, health care, cars, and just about everything else you spend money on, you need to set the initial distribution rate below your expected earnings on the capital so that you leave funds that can be reinvested. Your capital continues to grow throughout your retirement years to cover the larger amounts you'll need to withdraw later because of inflation.

When we look at all the historical cycles in the financial markets, going back to the 1920s, when investors tried to take out a 5% inflation-adjusted distribution, they were successful about 70% of the time in not running out of money over an assumed 30-year retirement. So there is a reasonably high probability that the money will last if you happen to live 30 years in retirement. But, it also means that about 30% of the time, investors could run out of money.

So, once retired, you need to use some common sense in how you manage distributions. If the stock market declines significantly, you may need to scale back your distributions to get through it. But, as the markets recover, you may be able to increase your distributions back to the 5% figure. In most cycles, this should work out just fine.

It also helps to have a sense of how you might have done at other distribution rates. That really puts the 5% number in perspective. Portfolios that dropped their distribution rate to 4% survived the 30-year hypothetical retirement cycles more than 95% of the time. But if you raise the rate to 6%, the success rate drops dramatically to only about 50%. That's risky territory when you're retired and totally dependent on your capital.

## A Margin for Error

What this research tells us is that the odds are pretty good that you can take an average of 5% of your capital per year in retirement and not run out of money. The reality, however, is that you will probably have varying distribution rates between 4% and 6% depending on how the markets perform. If things get tough, you may have to lower your rate to 4% for a year or two to get through a big bear market. And when things are good, you can comfortably do 5% and maybe even 6%.

> Example: If you happened to retire in 2000, you would have experienced two big bear markets in the first 10 years of your retirement cycle. Thus, you may be stuck at the 4% figure until the markets get better. But if you had retired in 1980, you could have easily done 6% because of the bull markets of the 1980s and 1990s. Timing is everything.

Remember, the markets usually provide positive long-term returns. So plan over the long term for the higher probability event, which is 5%, but be prepared to get through the lower probability event, which may require you to drop to 4%.

This is the reason that it is vital that you eliminate all debt before you retire: it gives you priceless flexibility. With no debt, you can shift your distribution rate down without creating stress in your budget. This allows you to get through a tough cycle without selling capital and to benefit when the markets recover. It's easy to cut back on luxuries, but debt payments are there no matter what you do. We'll talk more about this later.

If you experience an economic cycle where you need to be at 4%, the Capital to Income Ratio provides you with a margin of error to deal with these periods. At 12 times pay, you should be able to reach the 80% income replacement rate using the 5% distribution. If you go to a 4% distribution, where does that leave you with respect to your income replacement?

At 12 times pay, taking out 4% replaces 48% of your former

income. Add in Social Security of about 20%, and you are at 68%. If you are unlucky and experience a bad market cycle early in your retirement, you should still be fine at 68%. If you've done everything right, you will have no debt, won't be paying FICA taxes anymore, and won't need to be saving. The 68% may not be everything you hoped for, but it is still pretty good and will probably be quite comfortable.

The thing you have to recognize about retirement is that there are no guarantees. Your income will fluctuate with the economy. That's inevitable. The key is to build up enough capital such that you can withstand those fluctuations and position yourself for the good years.

Think about it this way: you have more certainty with your retirement income than with your job. You can lose your job at any time, and if you do it means a 100% decline in your income. But if you build capital, you can diversify your holdings. When markets are rough, you may see a decline in your income, but you'll still have enough capital available to produce income—income you get without having to work. In the "Investment Ratio" chapter, I will discuss strategies for diversifying and protecting your capital so you can enjoy this security.

## If You Fall Behind

What happens if you calculate your Capital to Income Ratio and discover that you don't have as much capital accumulated at a certain age as you should? This happens a lot, but there is a solution.

Example: We have Kevin and Amber, both 45, with $100,000 of household income. Kevin has $125,000 in his 401(k), Amber has $100,000 in her 401(k), and they have $25,000 in a brokerage account. Their total savings is $250,000. But according to the chart, their CIR should be 3.7, which means they should have $370,000 of savings. Therefore, they are $120,000 underfunded at this point in their lives.

In that type of situation, you have two choices. The first is to determine if you can catch up by age 65. For Kevin and Amber, if they wanted to catch up, they would need to save more to try to bring their CIR up each year. In this case, the couple would be required to save about 20% per year. If they can handle that, then this would be a good solution. With the additional savings, each year their CIR should be improving and they would be getting closer to their target. If they stick with it, by the time they reach age 65, their CIR should be at 12. (If you are behind in your CIR, you can go to my Web site, www.yourmoneyratios.com, and plug in your figures for an estimate of where you stand in your retirement plans; to get access to the calculator, enter the following code: 778811.)

But what if you don't think you can catch up? What if saving 20% of your income just isn't realistic? Can you do another 3%? In that case, it's more realistic for you to consider changing your retirement expectations. Instead of trying to retire on 80% of your income at age 65, you may find you are perfectly comfortable on 70% at age 65. Or, maybe you want to be at 70% but can wait until age 70 to retire. This gives you five more years to save and for the savings to grow.

These are all reasonable solutions to the situation. What would not be reasonable is to ignore where you are and not make any plans to get yourself to the point where you have some financial independence. The worst thing is to become discouraged and not take any positive steps. In the "Savings Ratio" chapter, you will find two other Capital to Income Ratio charts for people who might want to retire on just 70% of their income at age 65, or 70% at age 70. Once you take a look at your own finances, decide what is most realistic for you.

## Special Situations

Some readers will need to make adjustments to the Capital to Income Ratio because of certain special situations. There are four situations that require changes to your Capital to Income Ratio:

1. A company pension
2. An age difference of greater than 5 years between you and your spouse
3. A spouse who enters and exits the workforce periodically
4. Rapidly increasing income late in a person's career

If you fall into one of these categories, consult the "Special Situations" appendix, where I explain how to make some simple adjustments to the ratios to accommodate these circumstances.

# The Savings Ratio

Making money is only part of the equation. After you make it, you must save it. Remember, your savings is your source of investment capital to build your CIR. That is why developing the habit of saving is so critical. The irony is that the more you save today, the more you can spend later. Your savings will grow and actually *increase* your purchasing power later in life. It's like being a farmer of money: if you plant and grow your crop properly, you will be sitting on top of a lot of money come harvest time (also known as retirement) and have as much money to spend as a capitalist as you did as a laborer.

That's what is so sweet about being a capitalist: you have lots of money to spend and you can spend your time fishing, sketching paintings in the Louvre, or whatever else turns you on. But getting to that point requires discipline and good risk-management skills. If you develop those skills early, once you get there, you will have the ability to be a good capitalist. If you don't, you could end up wondering where all that money went. By now you may be asking, "OK, smart guy, how much should I be saving?" I thought you'd never ask.

## Working with the Savings Ratio

The Savings Ratio indicates how much of your income you should be saving each year to help you reach your CIR. Because our incomes tend to increase over time as we progress in our careers and our fixed expenses should be decreasing as we pay down our debts, we have two savings rates—one prior to age 45 and one after age 45. When you are under age 45, you should be saving at least 12% of your pay each year. After age 45, you should be saving 15% per year. If you can save more than those figures, that's wonderful. But at the absolute minimum, you must save 12% to age 45, and 15% beyond.

Remember, if you are following the Money Ratios, the percentage of your annual income that you must spend on paying your mortgage will be declining as you age. When you hit your mid 40s, you will have more room in your budget for savings because your mortgage cost is falling as a percentage of your pay. At this time, it should be comfortable for you to step your savings rate up to 15%.

The Savings Ratio is a pretax number. This means you take your total income and multiple it by the applicable Savings Ratio, and that is how much you should be saving each year. So if your gross income is $100,000 a year, you should be saving at least $12,000 per year prior to age 45 and $15,000 per year thereafter.

Most people find it easier to grasp this information when it's broken into monthly savings. Because the initial savings rate is 12%, for simplicity I will use 12% in the examples throughout this chapter. Obviously, the way to get your monthly savings number is to divide your annual savings number by 12. So if you make $100,000, you need to save at least $12,000 a year, or $1,000 per month— or if you're paid on a biweekly basis like most people, $500 from each paycheck. Smaller amounts seem to make the program more manageable.

## SAVINGS RATIO

| Age | Savings Ratio |
|-----|---------------|
| 25  | 12% |
| 30  | 12% |
| 35  | 12% |
| 40  | 12% |
| 45  | 15% |
| 50  | 15% |
| 55  | 15% |
| 60  | 15% |
| 65  | 15% |

If you save 12% of your pay every year, starting with your first year on the job, and you increase your rate to 15% after age 45, you should be hitting your desired CIR at each age. Ultimately, you should accumulate enough personal capital by age 65 such that the earnings on that capital are equal to about 60% of your preretirement. Add your Social Security benefit, which should be about 20% of your income, and you should be living a very comfortable lifestyle without needing to work.

We are using many long-term assumptions about financial market returns to calculate our figures, and because the assumptions are estimates and not guaranteed, it's smart to save more than 12% or 15% if you can. If you can't, that's fine, but my suggestion is that when possible, either because your pay increased or you kept your expenses low, you should try to save an extra 3% of income beyond the 12% or 15% minimum. Boosting your savings rate will help provide some insurance for your capital in the event that your returns are lower than projected. Later in the book, I'll show you how to use your 401(k) and employer match to help you get that extra 3% in your savings, just about every year.

## Profit and Discipline

When you think about it, savings is just like profit in a company. Profit serves as a source of investment capital for companies just like savings serves as the source of investment capital for individuals. Companies are organized around generating a profit. Their activities, sales, marketing, products, and costs are all organized to that end.

The reason many businesses are good at generating profits is because business systems impose discipline. If there was no discipline in business, you can be sure most businesses would fail. They would spend more than they earn and go under. No one really likes the discipline, but businesspeople realize they must live with it and know that, in the long run, it builds wealth. It is interesting to note that major corporations have a profit margin of about 10% to 12% of revenue. They operate their businesses at about the same profit margin you need to operate your household.

But when we get home, there is no discipline to family finances. There are no outsiders or investors analyzing what we do and pushing us to reach these goals. Nor do we have a stated common economic objective, as exists in a business. Therefore, it is harder to be disciplined. By incorporating a few business principles, such as a 12% savings/profit goal, and getting the family organized around that goal, you are imposing discipline. This discipline will make you happier and wealthier in the long run.

## Living on a Budget

Readers often say, "I can barely make ends meet now, how am I supposed to save 12% of my income?" In a word, *budgeting*. I debated whether or not to include material on budgeting in this book, because it diverges from the core material. But I decided that budgeting is such a pervasive issue for most people and such an obstacle to building all-important capital that it was too important not to discuss. So let's spend a few minutes talking about living on a budget.

Quite simply, if you are going to save at least 12% of your income each year, you need a budget. You cannot run your finances without one. In business, employees can't go around spending whatever they want whenever they want and somehow expect the company to make money. The same theory applies with your personal finances. You need a budget that helps you achieve the 12% savings goal.

Most people, however, hate to budget. They see it as something that restricts their freedom. That is the wrong way to approach budgeting. A budget is a positive undertaking that lays out the path for achieving your financial goals each year. Instead of using the term "budget," it is helpful to think of this process as your Capital Accumulation Plan (CAP). Your CAP is the road map for hitting your Money Ratios each year. It helps you estimate your budget, which identifies how much capital you can accumulate. The better you manage your income and expenses, the more capital you can create and the faster you can make your transformation from laborer to capitalist.

If you understand the importance of creating capital and the freedom it gives you, the CAP becomes a positive part of your daily life. A CAP creates clarity of purpose with your family finances and organizes your decisions around creating capital.

We all have a certain amount of slippage in our personal expenses.

There are things that we spend money on that we don't need or that we could get for less. Eliminating that slippage is one of the keys to capturing more capital. A good CAP should help you identify an extra 5% to 10% of salvageable capital each year. Considering that your goal is to accumulate at least 12% to 15%, you could achieve a major portion of your Savings Ratio simply by having a good CAP.

A CAP is nothing more than a monthly breakdown of all of your income and expenses, but it is incredibly important. A detailed CAP allows you to evaluate each item and determine if you need it or if you can get it for less. You can create a CAP by simply entering all of your income and expenses in a notebook or on a spreadsheet, or by using one of the many new software programs designed to help you keep track of your income and expenses. I have seen people do it successfully using each of these techniques. The key is to use one that you find easy and that you will consistently maintain.

Many of the new software programs for personal financial management are very user-friendly. They make the budgeting process easy because they can grab most of your income and expense items electronically from your bank account and credit card transactions. This is where most budgets fall apart. People get tired of entering all the data. But the new systems do about 95% of that work for you and present you with a pretty complete budget just by downloading your transactions. All you need to do is spend a small amount of time each month clarifying some of the categories and scrubbing a little of the data.

I expect you could shave 10% from your current spending simply by being diligent about what you spend and why you are spending it. But if you don't have a way of analyzing the numbers, all you are doing is guessing. Most people underestimate what they spend on all kinds of things. That is why they often don't have any capital left at the end of the month to save.

## Cutting Doesn't Mean Deprivation

Unless you have lost your job in the rocky economy, spending, not insufficient income, is your real problem. What makes this challenging is that cutting spending is painful. We get locked into a lifestyle and locked into debt that we can't pay off. Some folks feel that taking 12% off the top of their current income will cripple their lifestyle. But if you put your mind to it, there are many ways that you can trim 12% from your spending. It's important to remember that a small sacrifice in your spending today can produce a great benefit in the future.

Let's talk about cutting costs. Two big-ticket items that eat up a lot of income are home mortgages and cars, which we will talk about later in the "Debt Ratios" chapter. But there are many smaller expenses that can turn into a source of investment capital if you focus on reducing unnecessary spending. The point of budgeting is to get rid of those things that are costing you money but don't add a great deal of value to your life. This will be different for everybody because we all like to do different things. But the bottom line is, why pay extra for things you don't value but continue to spend money on because it's become a habit? If you're going to have discretionary spending, make it on things that you really value.

For instance, let's say you are an avid quilter. You want to spend money on quilting supplies and still save 12% of your income. Fine. Cut back in other areas that don't give you the same enjoyment or satisfaction. By cutting in the nonsatisfying areas, you can free up the cash to quilt and still meet your 12% savings goal. When removing some of these expenses, I recommend that you view it as a way to help you finance the things you want to do while still building adequate capital each year.

## Make Saving a Habit

The point of all this is to work on the habit of saving (or as I think of it, the habit of creating investment capital). It is critical to your success. Saving and not spending frivolously must become second nature to you. Squirrels do it. They know they've got to save food for the winter or they'll die. Our parents and grandparents had the "savings gene." Saving was survival to them, and there also wasn't as much cool stuff to buy during World War II. But today's consumption-heavy culture has beaten the savings habit out of many of us. You must *practice* saving just like you practice anything else you want to master. If you want to be a good golfer, you need to practice your swing so much so that it becomes second nature. You don't think about it. You just do it. Saving is the same way. You have to etch the practice into your psyche—to resist pulling out that credit card and instead ask, "Do I really need this?" Eventually, you will naturally make the smart decision, and over time, you will build investment capital. As you build your capital, you get a return on it. Eventually, that return will be large enough to replace your wages and you can retire. Saving is a means to a more comfortable future.

## Don't Forget Inflation

There are many assumptions built into the Savings Ratio. First, I assume you will be saving for a minimum of 40 years (ages 25 to 65), and that you will earn a return on your investments of about 4.5% after inflation. That means if inflation is 3.0%, you earned about 7.5% on your money. The 4.5% return is referred to as a "real rate" of return. This means the real growth in your purchasing power once we take inflation out of the picture. If you achieve a 4.5% real return on your money, then for each year that goes by, your purchasing power (the goods and services you can buy) goes up by 4.5%. This is why you invest. You save now so that you can spend more later.

> Example: Assume you want to buy an outfit that costs $100. You can buy the outfit today for $100, and that's it. Or you can invest the $100 for one year. If you invest the $100, and receive a 7.5% return, you have $107.50 next year. If inflation is 3.0%, next year the outfit will cost $103.00. But you have $107.50, so you have an extra $4.50 to spend. This is the 4.5% real rate of return. You can buy a yo-yo, a pretzel, or whatever you want. If your return outpaces inflation, which it should over the long term, by saving you are actually increasing your future lifestyle. Taking inflation out of the picture and measuring your real rate of return is a much better way to calculate the growth of your wealth. If you don't take inflation out of the returns, you can get some distorted numbers.

If your investments grow by 8% in a year, how much does your wealth actually increase? You don't know unless you figure out inflation. If inflation was 10%, as it was during certain periods of the 1970s, you actually lost money even though it looks like your assets grew. Using the same example, if the outfit costs $100 this year and inflation is 10%, that means the outfit will cost $110 next year. If you invested your $100 for a year and it grew by 8% to $108, you won't have enough to buy the same outfit you could have bought last year for $100. You have to take $2 from somewhere else to buy the same outfit a year later. Consequently, your wealth actually decreased. This is why you must always take inflation into account when creating your long-term financial picture and focus on your real rate of return.

The good news is that investment returns tend to maintain a certain spread above inflation over long periods of time. This is why people invest, so that their ability to buy more in the future increases. Our best source of information about what the future might hold for the financial markets is research on how the financial markets have performed in the past. While past performance is not a guarantee of future results, it is one of the most important pieces of data we have for estimating future financial returns.

When you look at all of those historical cycles, you see that a 4.5% real rate of return is a prudent long-term assumption for a balanced, diversified portfolio. This means that if inflation is 3.0%, financial market returns might be 7.5%. Or, if inflation is 2.0%, financial market returns might be 6.5%. Therefore, when planning for retirement, I assume your savings will grow by a 4.5% real return over the 40-year cycle. During some periods you may do better, and during some you'll do worse, but over a 40-year cycle of savings and investing, this is a fair assumption regarding the potential growth of your capital.

It is important to use long-term numbers because if we focus on a short cycle, then we may use numbers that are either too optimistic or too pessimistic. Being too optimistic may cause you to save too little, while being too pessimistic may restrict your lifestyle so much that you can't follow through on the goals.

If I had suggested this 4.5% real return number in the late 1990s, you may have thought that I was being much too conservative, given that the markets had been pumping out 20% or higher returns for years and inflation was below 3%, delivering "real" returns of more than 15% for many years. But after the last few years, many may feel that 4.5% is too optimistic considering the huge declines in the financial markets. That is why you need to look beyond the most immediate cycle and get a sense of the longer-term trends. We will talk about this more in the "Investment Ratio" chapter, but good cycles are usually followed by bad cycles, and bad cycles by good cycles. When you average it all out over a 40-year period, the annualized numbers fall in between the dramatic highs and lows, which is why the 4.5% real return is a prudent assumption.

## The Income Replacement Charts

Earlier, I introduced the Capital to Income Ratio. I am now going to add the Savings Ratio to the mix and you can see how the pieces start coming together in the Money Ratios. As we go through each chapter, I will be adding new ratios for debt, investments, and insurance to the chart, and it will be easy to see how each piece fits into the puzzle.

Because the Savings Ratio and Capital to Income Ratio are designed to allow you to retire at age 65 on 80% of your preretirement income, the following chart is the Age 65 & 80% Income Replacement Chart. Later charts are the Age 65 & 70% Income Replacement Chart and the Age 70 & 70% Income Replacement Chart. Each is labeled by an anticipated retirement age and an Income Replacement Ratio. This allows you to assess where you are today and which objective is most realistic going forward.

| Age 65 & 80% Income Replacement | | |
|---|---|---|
| *Age* | *Capital to Income Ratio* | *Savings Ratio* |
| 25 | 0.1 | 12% |
| 30 | 0.6 | 12% |
| 35 | 1.4 | 12% |
| 40 | 2.4 | 12% |

| Age | Capital to Income Ratio | Savings Ratio |
|-----|-------------------------|---------------|
| 45  | 3.7                     | 15%           |
| 50  | 5.2                     | 15%           |
| 55  | 7.1                     | 15%           |
| 60  | 9.4                     | 15%           |
| 65  | 12.0                    | 15%           |

Each year you are converting a part of your wages (12% to 15%) into personal capital. That capital grows over the years, and your objective is to reach age 65 with capital equal to at least 12 times your pay. All you need to do is identify your age and run your income figures against the ratios. If you were age 40 making $100,000 a year, you need to be saving $12,000 a year, and you should have total savings worth $240,000 at your age.

## The Secret of Two Times Pay

If you look at your retirement account, you might be wondering how you will ever get to 12 times pay. You might be doing a quick calculation in your head thinking that if you save 12% of pay each year, it will take roughly eight years to get to one times pay. If you need to do that 12 times, you will need 96 years' worth of savings! But you don't need 96 years of savings. You only need about 35 to 40 years.

The reason is you have a partner in your journey from laborer to capitalist called *compound earnings*. Over your lifetime, the odds are the compound earnings on your money will actually add far more than you will add through your savings each year. In the beginning that doesn't seem to be the case, but your finances hit a tipping point at about two times pay. After you have saved two times your pay, the earnings from your capital will generally add more to your total wealth than the amount you save each year. This is when your wealth starts to accelerate. Your focus should be on getting to two times pay. Once you reach that point, you will see positive results much faster.

> Example: Assume you earn $100,000 a year and are saving
> 12% of pay. In your first year of savings you add $12,000 to
> your retirement account. You get a 7.5% return on that money,
> which is $900. Thus, you added $12,000 through your savings
> and your savings added $900 through its earnings. The total
> addition to your personal capital that year was $12,900. At this
> point in your life, your savings rate has the biggest impact on
> your wealth.

Now assume you have been saving for about 10 years and you have $200,000 in your retirement plan, or two times your annual pay. If you get a 7.5% return, the earnings are $15,000. This exceeds your savings of $12,000. In this year, your wealth increased by $27,000, and more than half of that came from earnings on your capital. After this point, the earnings will be the biggest contributor and your CIR should begin to grow very quickly.

Think about what happens when you are at six times pay, or $600,000. You are still saving $12,000 a year, but your earnings at 7.5% would be $45,000. Now you've added a total of $57,000 to your capital in one year, which is the equivalent of almost five years' worth of savings. This is the amazing thing about capital: it creates more capital. The more you have, the easier it is to accumulate more.

Over a 40-year savings cycle, your ending account value will likely consist of about 30% contributions and 70% earnings on those contributions. That is the incredible power of compound growth on your capital. If you end up saving $1,000,000 for retirement, the odds are about $300,000 or so will consist of your capital, while the other $700,000 will be the earnings on that capital. That is why you should not be intimidated by the large CIR figures. You don't have to contribute all of that money into your retirement plan. You only have to do about 30% of it, and the financial markets should help with the rest.

## Retiring at 65 on 70% of Income

As I mentioned before, it's possible that you are behind in your savings and the age 65 & 80% retirement goals appear too hard to reach. To address this common situation, I have developed an Income Replacement chart for retiring at age 65 on 70% income replacement. Remember, you were probably living on 70% or even 60% of your total income prior to retirement, which means you may find this to be a comfortable goal. If your goal is 70% income replacement, then you only have to reach 10 times pay by age 65, instead of 12. At 10 times pay, using a 5% distribution rate, you should be generating 50% of your preretirement income from your investment earnings. Add the anticipated 20% from Social Security, and you should be at 70% income replacement. The lower capital accumulation goal means that you can save less each year, but you must be willing to live on less in retirement.

To get to 10 times pay by age 65, the Savings Ratio falls to 10% prior to age 45 and 13% thereafter (as opposed to 12% and 15%). You can also see in the chart below that the Capital to Income Ratio is smaller at each age. You may run your ratios and find out that you are closer to the 70% income replacement path than the 80%

income replacement path. If you can, ramp up your savings to get on track for the 80% goal, but if you cannot, then the 70% might work well for you. The point of the different charts is to help you understand that there are multiple ways to climb the mountain and move from laborer to capitalist.

| Age 65 & 70% Income Replacement | | |
|---|---|---|
| Age | Capital to Income Ratio | Savings Ratio |
| 25 | 0.1 | 10% |
| 30 | 0.5 | 10% |
| 35 | 1.25 | 10% |
| 40 | 2.0 | 10% |
| 45 | 3.1 | 13% |
| 50 | 4.5 | 13% |
| 55 | 6.1 | 13% |
| 60 | 8.1 | 13% |
| 65 | 10.0 | 13% |

The following chart compares the Age 65 & 80% Ratio with the Age 65 & 70% Ratio. As you review both savings programs, be careful about using the lower Income Replacement chart. It is difficult to predict what you will need in retirement, so the higher your CIR, the better. If, however, you are having trouble staying on track for the 80% replacement rate, then at least strive for the 70% figure and improve your savings as your finances permit.

| Age | Age 65 & 80% Income Replacement | | Age 65 & 70% Income Replacement | |
| --- | --- | --- | --- | --- |
| | Capital to Income Ratio | Savings Ratio | Capital to Income Ratio | Savings Ratio |
| 25 | 0.1 | 12% | 0.1 | 10% |
| 30 | 0.6 | 12% | 0.5 | 10% |
| 35 | 1.4 | 12% | 1.25 | 10% |
| 40 | 2.4 | 12% | 2.0 | 10% |
| 45 | 3.7 | 15% | 3.1 | 13% |
| 50 | 5.2 | 15% | 4.5 | 13% |
| 55 | 7.1 | 15% | 6.1 | 13% |
| 60 | 9.4 | 15% | 8.1 | 13% |
| 65 | 12.0 | 15% | 10.0 | 13% |

Now let's take another look at Kevin and Amber, the 45-year-old couple with $100,000 of income and $250,000 of savings. If they want to use the Age 65 & 70% Income Replacement Chart, their Capital to Income Ratio should be 3.1, which means they should have $310,000 of savings. With $250,000 of savings they are slightly underfunded by $60,000, which isn't too bad. They should be able to catch up over the next few years, which means they can at least get on track for a 70% income replacement. This couple would need to save about 15% of their pay for the next 20 years to get to the Capital to Income Ratio of 10 by age 65. This may be much more achievable than the 20% rate required if they want to get to 12 times income by age 65.

## Retiring at 70 on 70% of Income

Maybe you're behind in your savings but love your job, so you don't have any burning need to retire at age 65. What about retiring at age 70 on 70% of your income? For the 70% income replacement, you need a CIR of 10, but you don't need it until age 70, which means you could get by with a slightly lower Savings Ratio of 8% prior to age 45 and 10% thereafter because you have 5 more years of savings and compounding.

| Age 70 & 70% Income Replacement | | |
|---|---|---|
| *Age* | *Capital to Income Ratio* | *Savings Ratio* |
| 25 | 0.1 | 8% |
| 30 | 0.45 | 8% |
| 35 | 1.0 | 8% |
| 40 | 1.6 | 8% |
| 45 | 2.5 | 10% |
| 50 | 3.5 | 10% |
| 55 | 4.8 | 10% |
| 60 | 6.5 | 10% |
| 65 | 8.2 | 10% |
| 70 | 10.0 | 10% |

As I mentioned before, be careful about lowering your objectives for your retirement income. While it might look easier to hit these ratios, you will be required to work and save for another 5 years. But you cannot count on always being healthy enough to work full-time. Even small changes in your health status can make it difficult to continue with a full work schedule. Thus, there are added risks to pushing your retirement date back 5 years and also shooting for a lower Capital to Income Ratio.

When markets are tough you may need to drop your distribution rate to 4%. If you have a Capital to Income Ratio of 10, a 4% distribution is a 40% income replacement rate. Add in the assumed Social Security, and you are at 60%. Thus, if you aim for the lower ratio, be prepared to manage through a cycle that may require you to live on only 60% of your preretirement income. It may not happen, but if it does, you need to be able to handle it.

For some people, however, the lower ratios may be the most realistic goal because you might not have a high enough Capital to Income Ratio at your age to hit 12 times pay at 65. Therefore, put yourself on track for the 10 times pay at age 65 or 70, and add as much additional capital as you can if finances improve. You may find that you are able to close the gap faster if you get some good market returns or your pay jumps significantly. In either event, keep pushing ahead. You might be heading down the laborer to capitalist path a little slower than you like, but you will get there.

If we go back to our hypothetical 45-year-old couple, Kevin and Amber, with $100,000 of income and $250,000 of savings, we can benchmark them against the Age 70 & 70% Replacement Chart. At age 45, their Capital to Income Ratio should be 2.5, which means they should have $250,000. This couple has $250,000 of savings, so they know they are on track for at least an age 70 and 70% income replacement at retirement. With some additional determination, maybe they can start to close the gap on the age 65 and 70% or even the age 65 and 80% goals.

## Pulling It All Together

Go to my Web site, www.yourmoneyratios.com, and plug your numbers into my calculator using the code: 778811. The calculator will give you an estimate of where you are in relation to the age 65 and 80%, age 65 and 70%, or age 70 and 70% scenarios. The calculator helps you to see which path you are on. I assume a 4.5% real rate of return, but if it is lower, the only solution is to save more. If it is higher, you may be able to retire early.

To summarize, we have three different Income Replacement Charts. I call them the Gold, Silver, and Bronze standards for retirement. The Gold Standard is to retire at age 65 on 80% of your preretirement income. The Silver Standard is to retire at age 65 on 70% of your preretirement income. And the Bronze Standard is to retire at age 70 on 70% of your preretirement income. The following chart summarizes the options.

### RETIREMENT INCOME OPTIONS

| Age | Age 65 & 80% Income Replacement | | Age 65 & 70% Income Replacement | | Age 70 & 70% Income Replacement | |
|---|---|---|---|---|---|---|
| | Capital to Income Ratio | Savings Ratio | Capital to Income Ratio | Savings Ratio | Capital to Income Ratio | Savings Ratio |
| 25 | 0.1 | 12% | 0.1 | 10% | 0.1 | 8% |
| 30 | 0.6 | 12% | 0.5 | 10% | 0.45 | 8% |
| 35 | 1.4 | 12% | 1.25 | 10% | 1.0 | 8% |
| 40 | 2.4 | 12% | 2.0 | 10% | 1.6 | 8% |

| Age | Age 65 & 80% Income Replacement | | Age 65 & 70% Income Replacement | | Age 70 & 70% Income Replacement | |
|---|---|---|---|---|---|---|
| | *Capital to Income Ratio* | *Savings Ratio* | *Capital to Income Ratio* | *Savings Ratio* | *Capital to Income Ratio* | *Savings Ratio* |
| 45 | 3.7 | 15% | 3.1 | 13% | 2.5 | 10% |
| 50 | 5.2 | 15% | 4.5 | 13% | 3.5 | 10% |
| 55 | 7.1 | 15% | 6.1 | 13% | 4.8 | 10% |
| 60 | 9.4 | 15% | 8.1 | 13% | 6.5 | 10% |
| 65 | 12.0 | 15% | 10.0 | 13% | 8.2 | 10% |
| 70 | X | X | X | X | 10.0 | 10% |

If you save more, you are building more capital early on. With more capital, the compound earnings on that money propel you faster from laborer to capitalist. If you are going to take away one idea from this book, it should be to build as much capital as early as you can and whenever you can. That is the key to the game. Next time you get a raise, a bonus, or are fortunate enough to get an inheritance, think about what you want to do with that money. The quicker it becomes a part of your personal capital, the faster you will progress from laborer to capitalist.

Calculate your current Capital to Income Ratio for your age. Then, consult the chart to determine whether you are closest to the Gold, Silver, or Bronze retirement. This will give you a sense of the path you are on. The key is to stay in the game and keep playing. There are lots of good things that can happen as long as you continue to add capital and consistently improve your ratios.

# 3

# Social Security

Social Security is crucial to your retirement security. Yet when I ask people about Social Security, many roll their eyes and proclaim that they don't believe they will get a Social Security benefit. From a personal and public policy standpoint, this is terrible. The fact that people have lost so much confidence in the system speaks to the need to educate people about Social Security. Because the simple truth is, unless you are part of a very small percentage of high-net-worth individuals, you will need Social Security to reach your retirement income goals.

First of all, the system is quite secure for the next 20 or 30 years, but there are longer-term issues that require us to act sooner rather than later. I think that after reading this chapter you will come to appreciate how important Social Security is to your retirement, have confidence that it will be there, and support policies and elected officials who want to reform and maintain the integrity of Social Security, the most successful entitlement program this country has ever created.

Social Security was created by Franklin Delano Roosevelt's administration during the Great Depression as a solution to the poverty that afflicted many elderly citizens. The program is actually called the Old-Age, Survivors, and Disability Insurance program, or OASDI. It is designed to provide benefits to people who are old, widows, and those who are disabled. Prior to Social Security, there was no social safety net. Everyone needed to fend for themselves and many could not manage to do so, especially during the Depression.

Social Security is a marvelous concept. It provides a basic government guarantee for retirement income and provides some basic financial benefits to our families if we should die young or become disabled. The difficulty comes, as it does with any long-term social program, in anticipating and planning for the changes that take place within our society.

## How It Works

Most people who work are covered by the Social Security system. You qualify for benefits based on the number of covered quarters (three-month periods) you work in a sector of the economy that qualifies for Social Security. Basically, if you have worked more than 10 years in covered employment, you generally are fully qualified for benefits. Those benefits are based on a very complicated formula that is tied to your years of work and total average earnings during those years.

There are some workers who are not covered by Social Security. Generally, they work for a state or local government organization or agency. A few government employers are exempt from contributing to Social Security, but they operate their own retirement programs designed to provide a retirement benefit for their employees. Most people who are not covered by Social Security are well aware of it. If you work for an employer that was not part of Social Security, but also work for employers that were, and you earn enough service credits to qualify for Social Security, you may be subject to the "windfall elimination provision." This provision cuts back on a part of your Social Security benefit because you are also getting a retirement benefit from the employer that was not part of Social Security.

Every year, you receive a Social Security statement near your birthday. It provides a history of your earnings and an estimate of your benefit—assuming you continue to work. This is an important document because it records your eligibility for the program and the earnings on which the benefit will be based. The goal of the report is to help people understand what their benefits might be and to raise awareness about the program.

The Social Security retirement date is somewhere between age 65 and 67, depending on when you were born. If you were born before 1937, your full retirement age is 65. For those born between 1938 and 1959, their full retirement age is between 65 and 67. For those born in 1960 or later, full retirement age is 67. You can start collecting Social Security benefits as early as age 62, but they will be reduced. The benefits are designed so that whether you take benefits early or later, you should end up with the same total amount. But it's up to you to make a decision about your Social Security start date based on your individual circumstances.

You will notice on each paycheck that you have a deduction for FICA taxes. That is your part of Social Security in action. You contribute to the Social Security program through the FICA tax system. FICA is the law that establishes the taxes to fund Social Security and Medicare. The bulk of those taxes goes to Social Security, with some also going to Medicare. In 2010, FICA taxes were applied to your first $106,800 of wages. This is called the wage base, and it is indexed for inflation each year. You pay one half of the FICA tax, and your employer pays the other half. The Social Security part of the FICA tax is 12.4%. You pay 6.2%, and your employer makes a 6.2% contribution when filing payroll taxes each month. Thus, you are putting an enormous amount of money into the system each year.

The total FICA tax is 7.65% of wages from you, plus another 7.65% of wages from your employer, for a total of 15.3% on your first $106,800 of wages in 2010. Of the total, 12.4% goes to Social Security and 2.9% goes to Medicare. You pay FICA taxes on wages, but you do not pay them on your investment income (interest, dividends, and distributions from your IRA or 401(k)). This is why your total tax rate drops in retirement, because you no longer have to pay the FICA tax.

Your benefits are calculated on your annual earnings, up to the maximum wage base each year, and the total number of years you worked. So if you make $150,000 a year, your FICA tax is paid on your first $106,800, and your benefit is based on that $106,800 wage base, not the $150,000 you earned. Thus, your Social Security benefit has a ceiling.

The benefit formula is structured so that the lower your career earnings, the higher the income replacement rate is. For instance, if your average earnings were $50,000 a year, your Social Security benefit as a percentage of pay will be higher than someone who averaged $100,000 a year. Lower-paid workers could see replacement rates as high as 50%, while higher-paid workers hover around 25%.

If you are married, your spouse has a right to Social Security benefits equal to the higher of his or her own benefit or one half of yours. Assuming your spouse did not work at all, and your replacement rate is 25%, you could add another 12.5% for your spouse, which would put you at 37.5% income replacement. If your spouse did work, the replacement rate would be higher. Another terrific thing about Social Security is that it is adjusted for inflation. This is a big deal, because the benefit will grow as you age, and help you maintain a constant purchasing power and quality of life.

If you and your spouse make substantially more than $106,800 each, your Social Security will replace a smaller percentage of your total wages. This is because the benefit formula only counts your first $106,800 of wages, because you are only making Social Security contributions on $106,800. Thus, the wages you earn above that amount are not subject to

Social Security contributions and consequently not eligible to be included in the benefit formula.

## Change Is Inevitable

My assumption that Social Security will replace about 20% of your household income in retirement is a conservative estimate for the vast majority of families. One of the most important things to note is that while I am quite confident that Social Security will be there for people retiring 30, 40, and 50 years from now, I am also confident that there will be changes. Life expectancy is simply increasing too quickly and the baby boom generation is simply too large to allow the program to continue without systemic change. I hope it does not happen, but the reality is that some payout cuts are likely. If those cuts can be smaller to maintain the program, that is infinitely better than doing nothing until it runs out of money.

This is a question I hear often: If we are putting all this money into Social Security, why should we anticipate cuts? First, understand that Social Security as a program is a good idea. It requires all of us to contribute to one large retirement plan. Because there are millions of people of different ages and incomes contributing to the program, the Social Security system has a strong and consistent funding stream. This gives the system the financial strength to guarantee each of us a basic retirement benefit. Your Social Security benefit serves as a good hedge in case you don't get to save as much as you thought you could, or the markets turn ugly during your retirement. The Social Security payment is not based on how the markets do each year, so it is a good, conservative hedge for a part of your retirement income.

But like many good ideas, it has grown into a bit of a financial monster, for the simple reason that politicians like to grant—and voters like to get—more benefits without adequately funding those benefits. That is the basic problem. Over the years, the financial benefits from Social Security have expanded, but the funding of these benefits has not kept pace, in great part due to the American aversion to higher taxes even when they are in our best interest. At the present time, the Social Security program is in good shape. According to the 2009 Social Security Trust Fund report, the program is funded through 2037, and there are currently no plans to reduce benefits. But thereafter, we may have some problems.

After 2037, the current estimate is that Social Security will only have enough funding to pay about 76% of the scheduled benefits. If there are no changes, the Social Security Administration estimates that someone who is 37 years old in 2009 would need to anticipate a 24% reduction in benefits by retirement age, while someone who is 26 in 2009 might have to anticipate a 26% reduction. My estimates factor in even larger cuts for the average worker because I want to be more conservative in the figures.

The good news is that there is plenty of time to get ahead of the Social Security funding problem and fix it. The problem can be solved because we can predict the obligations of Social Security with a reasonable degree of accuracy. Thus, we can calculate how much needs to be put into the program. For example, the 2009 Trust Fund Report estimates that the Social Security funding problem could be fixed with an immediate 13% reduction in benefits, or an increase in the payroll tax of about another 2%, or some combination of the two. So we know what the numbers are and how much it will cost. The question is, do we have the political will to do it and do it fairly? Congress tends to want to put off dealing with the funding issues, and the average voter is happy to delay the debate as well. But the earlier we start, the easier it will be to fix.

## Understanding the Essentials

These are very important issues for your retirement security, and we all have an interest in addressing the problems while they are still small enough to fix. There are a number of potential solutions, which may include reducing some benefits, pushing back the retirement age, increasing contribution amounts, or some combination of all three. But most Americans need to feel that any solution is fundamentally fair. We will all likely need to compromise somewhat, but if we take a long-term perspective, I am confident we can come to an agreement on the solutions.

The danger, however, is that Congress resorts to a "class warfare" approach to fixing the problem, whereby it continues to tax higher wage earners more while reducing their benefits to fund the retirements of lower wage earners. There is already a good amount of wealth transfer built into the system. Currently, lower-paid workers get much more out of the system than higher-paid workers, based on their actual contributions. I think most people are all right with some aspect of the program being a wealth transfer. We are a rich nation, and we don't want elderly people living in poverty. Reasonable minds can differ on the subsidies to be provided to those with lower incomes, but there is a risk that we will go beyond providing a safety net and turn the system into a larger wealth-transfer program.

If tax rates and benefit structures are changed to increase taxes primarily on higher wage earners, while at the same time lowering their benefits, this will undermine the legitimacy of the entire program. Basically, higher wage earners would be putting in more and getting less, but lower wage earners would be putting in less and getting more. There needs to be a direct link between what you put in and what you get out. Otherwise, it becomes a welfare program and no longer a retirement program. This is why it is important for everyone to understand the basics of Social Security, how much they are putting into it, and how their basic benefits are calculated. You should be interested in ensuring that your benefits are based predominantly on what you contributed to the system.

Compare the Social Security contribution to the Savings Ratio numbers. Remember that I suggest you save 12% of income prior to age 45 and 15% thereafter to put you in a position to generate about 60% of your preretirement income from your capital. Most people make less than the Social Security wage base of $106,800 and thus are contributing another 12.4% of pay into this program. Yet the anticipated benefit from Social Security is nowhere near the 60% rate that you anticipate you can generate on your own capital.

One reason for this is that the money is not invested in the financial markets. This reduces the potential return. Also, about 1% of the total contribution goes to fund disability benefits, which reduces some of the return. The program is designed to be more conservative and provide a safety net, so we should expect that the income replacement rate would be lower than what we could get on our own. But another major reason the replacement rate is low is that a good amount of the money contributed into the plan is transferred from one set of workers to another. Nobody has an individual account.

If you are working, people who are receiving benefits today are essentially getting their benefits not from what they contributed, but from the funds you are contributing every month. This is called a "pay as you go" system, and it is highly dependent on demographics— having more workers than retirees. But the demographics of the United States are changing, and this is why we are likely to have funding shortfalls in the future. We will have too few workers contributing into the system to pay the bumper crop of new retirees.

You may have heard about the Social Security trust fund. Well, there is actually a fund into which all the contributions are made. Since the contributions are more than the amounts currently being paid out, there is an excess, and this makes up the trust fund. But the excess doesn't last. The Treasury Department borrows the excess each year and issues the trust fund treasury bonds for the amount borrowed. So the money is there in the form of Treasury debt. But that trust fund will be depleted over the years as distributions exceed contributions with more people retiring.

Underlying all of this is a structural problem with Social Security:

you don't have a contractual right to a Social Security benefit. This means you have no ownership in the money that is going into the program. Congress can change the law and your benefit amount at any time. This is why class warfare is dangerous. Congress can decide to pit one class of workers against another by making legislative changes that sweep away benefits for some workers and grant more benefits to others. The unintended consequences are that this could ignite a backlash against Social Security and jeopardize the long-term viability of a program that is important to all of us.

## Fair to Everyone

At the end of the day, people need to pay their fair share for benefits they receive from the government. Again, we can debate what is fair, but the fact is that we already have a healthy amount of wealth transfer going on. But if we further distance the benefit from any payment, we will have problems. If those who don't pay as much into the program insist on receiving more benefits, they can get them only by imposing a greater burden on those who do pay. This is not a healthy system. Just as with *Your Money Ratios*, the numbers need to be kept in proportion for each retiree, regardless of income.

The status of Social Security isn't something that should keep you up at night. Remember, the system is well funded for the next 27 years, and we know about the estimated shortfalls down the road. Furthermore, there is a great deal of interest in finding an equitable solution. But it is something to pay attention to and to encourage Congress to deal with sooner rather than later. Getting ahead of the problem will give the country time to make smaller changes and see what the effects are. If some of the changes don't work well, new ones can be implemented. If some do work well, we can do more of the same. But if we wait too long, until the system is in crisis, we will be forced into rash decisions that could harm everyone.

Personally, I think the system needs to institute some form of a private account. What I mean by this is that the law needs to be changed so that you have a property interest in some part of your Social Security contributions. It just doesn't seem fair that there is a risk that you could contribute hundreds of thousands of dollars into the program and have it legislated away. For instance, we could modify the law to state that you have a right to receive back 80% (plus inflation) of what you contributed in the form of a monthly retirement benefit. This at least gives you a property right in your basic contributions and adds legitimacy to the system. You could have confidence that the bulk of your contributions will come to you in the future, and maybe more.

Having some property rights to the benefits doesn't mean privatizing the system and letting people invest their own money. I don't think this would be a good idea, because it is important for us to have a portion of our money hedged against the vagaries of the financial markets. We have seen what can happen when we have blind faith in the financial markets. Thus, the government would keep the money, but it would be in an account with your name on it, and your benefits would be determined partially by how much you contributed to your account.

Right now, you have no "account"—just an earnings history. That earnings history is used to calculate benefits, but you have no right to the promised benefit. We don't allow this in the private pension world, and we shouldn't allow it in Social Security. The solution to Social Security should be some combination of small benefit reductions, small tax increases, slight adjustments to retirement ages, and the institution of some property rights to one's lifetime contributions. This way, everybody gives up a bit, but the system ends up healthier in the long run, which is good for all of us.

In summary, I think you can be confident that your Social Security benefit will be there when you retire, and that it will constitute 20% or more of your preretirement income. That is too vital a sum of money to dismiss with an "Oh, it won't be there when I retire." Social Security is one of the most important and successful programs run by the government. It would be a shame to let the financial underpinnings erode and cause people to lose confidence in the system. Stay informed about what is happening with Social Security. Read your annual benefit statement so you have an estimate of how much you will receive. Encourage your elected representatives to deal with the problem sooner rather than later. And keep in mind solutions that allow us to maintain the basic structure, but adequately and fairly fund it from the contributions of all Americans.

## Excluding Social Security Estimates

Some people feel strongly that they do not want to count on any Social Security benefit when calculating their sources of income for retirement. This is completely up to you. If you don't believe you will receive any benefit, then exclude the number. From a ratios standpoint, if you exclude Social Security, you need to increase your Capital to Income Ratio. If you want to reach an 80% income replacement rate, you must reach a Capital to Income Ratio of 16 instead of 12.

Social Security constitutes an estimated 20% of retirement income, so if you remove that source of income, you then need another 4 times the pay in savings to make up for the 20% loss, assuming the 5% distribution rate.

To reach a Capital to Income Ratio of 16 by age 65, you must increase your Savings Ratio to 18% of pay before age 45 and 20% of pay after age 45, as opposed to the 12% to 15% Savings Ratios if you include a basic Social Security benefit. If you can afford to save at these higher amounts and exclude any Social Security benefit from your calculations, this is a terrific goal. I'm all for more savings and more financial independence. But if you can't, then it's still reasonable to estimate a Social Security benefit of 20% of pay, because that estimate already includes a significant reduction in benefits from the current formulas.

# 4

# Where to Save Your Money

Now that you know how much you should be saving, where should you put your money? You have three primary options:

1. 401(k) plan
2. Individual Retirement Account (IRA)
3. Taxable investment account

I've listed them in order of importance and ease of use. You should put your savings in your 401(k) first, then an IRA (if tax laws allow it), and then a taxable investment account. And no matter which one, or combination you use, the savings must be automatic. You will be amazed at how fast you accumulate funds if you just put the savings on autopilot.

## The 401(k)

There are three reasons for using your 401(k) plan as your primary savings vehicle:

1. It imposes discipline—the savings is automatically removed from your pay.
2. It saves you taxes, which makes it easier to reach your savings goal.
3. If you have your employer match contributions, it helps you build more capital more quickly.

A 401(k) plan derives from section 401(k) of the Internal Revenue Code. Under that section of the tax law, there is a provision that allows employees to put a portion of their wages into an employer-sponsored retirement plan each year. When you elect to put a portion of your pay into a 401(k) plan, the funds are removed from your wages on a pretax basis. The money must generally remain invested until at least age 59½, at which time you can begin to take distributions for retirement. If you take a distribution from your retirement plan prior to age 59½, you must pay a 10% penalty tax and then ordinary income tax. All of these taxes can eliminate close to half of the money in the plan. So, it is important to make sure that money you put in a 401(k) stays there until you retire.

Also, if you leave your job prior to retirement, which many people do, you have the ability to roll over your 401(k) money to an IRA, which you own and control. You can do all of this without paying any tax on the money and continue to keep it invested for your retirement years. When you roll it over to an IRA, you have the same 59½ age restriction for distributions, which is why you don't have to pay a penalty tax or any income tax on the rollover. You are maintaining your commitment to keep the funds invested until you retire.

Alternatively, if you join a new employer, you can also consider rolling your 401(k) from your old employer to your new employer's plan. This can also be done without paying any tax. The bottom line is that there are a number of different options available to roll over and keep control of your retirement funds once you leave an employer, without having to pay the penalty tax or any income tax.

Only employers may establish 401(k) plans, and the money they hold is very secure. The funds are held for your benefit and are required by law to be completely segregated from the assets of your employer. The funds are maintained in a trust that is exempt from your creditors and any of your employer's creditors. This means that if you get into financial trouble, or your employer goes bankrupt, the assets in the retirement plan are completely safe. The reason there is so much protection is that the government wants to encourage people to use these plans to build retirement assets.

If you are self-employed, you can establish a solo 401(k), a simplified employee pension (SEP IRA), or a profit-sharing plan. You will need the assistance of your accountant and a pension expert, but once they are up and running, they offer similar opportunities for tax-deductible contributions and protection from creditors. When you put money in a 401(k) plan, you generally also have the right to manage those funds yourself. This creates the opportunity to have the money handled as you see fit. We will cover all these special situations later in the book.

## Making It Automatic

401(k) plans are unique because the funds are automatically deducted from your paycheck and placed directly into your retirement plan. You don't even have to think about it. Making savings easy—and taking away the temptation to spend the money one month and promise to "save twice as much" next month—is one of the keys to reaching your Savings Ratio. Because the contribution limits on 401(k) plans are relatively high, many people can reach their savings goal by simply using the automatic savings features of their 401(k) plan.

The annual contribution limits for 401(k) plans are tied to your age. In 2010, for people under age 50, the limit is $16,500. For people age 50 and over, the limit is $22,000. The IRS allows people

50 or older to contribute more so they can "catch up" later in life on their savings goals. The 401(k) limits are adjusted for inflation and will rise over time. The IRS publishes the new figures before the beginning of each year.

If you are under age 50 and want to save 15% of your income a year, the $16,500 limit allows everyone who makes up to $110,000 a year to contribute their entire 15% savings goal into a 401(k) (15% of $110,000 = $16,500). If you are over age 50 and you want to save 15% a year, then the $22,000 limit allows everyone who makes up to $146,666 a year to contribute their entire 15% savings goal into a 401(k) (15% of $146,666 is $22,000). As I said in the "Savings Ratio" chapter, you should bump up your savings rate to 15% after age 45. As you increase your savings rate later in your career, the higher limits will allow you to put more of those savings in your 401(k) plan.

One important item to understand about 401(k) contribution limits is that they are *per person*, not per household. So if you have two working spouses, each spouse has the option to put the maximum amount in his or her 401(k). If you and your spouse are both under age 50, you can save a maximum of $33,000 for 2009; if you are both over age 50, the maximum is $44,000. This is helpful if your household savings goal exceeds the maximum that you could put into a single 401(k) plan, because you can use both 401(k) plans to get the full amount.

Example: Assume we have a 45-year-old couple who each earn $75,000 a year, for a total of $150,000. Their 15% savings goal is $22,500 a year. If only one spouse was working and making $150,000, the 401(k) contribution limit would be only $16,500, $6,000 short of the goal. But because both are working and have 401(k) plans, they can save their entire $22,500 by using both plans and putting in 15% of pay, or $11,250, into each 401(k) plan.

Once you have maximized your 401(k) contribution (and bravo if you have done so), any additional savings should go to either an IRA or to a taxable investment account. All of these investment accounts offer the ability to implement an automatic savings feature. The 401(k) works through your employer payroll system. If you have an IRA or taxable brokerage account, you can establish an automatic transfer every month from your checking account.

## 401(k) Tax Savings

The automatic savings aspect of the 401(k) is great, but the primary reason you should use it is because of the tax savings. Saving on taxes will help build your capital much faster. Let's assume you want to save $10,000 for the year ($10,000 makes the examples easier to understand). When you contribute money to a 401(k) plan, that money is excluded from your income for purposes of calculating your federal income tax. It is also generally excluded from your income for purposes of state income taxes. That means you don't have to pay income taxes on the money and can put the full $10,000 right into your retirement plan. If you had to pay taxes on that income, then you would have less available for savings, which of course makes it harder to accumulate capital.

If your income tax bracket is a combined 25% from federal, state, and local income taxes, this means you would pay $2,500 of taxes on that $10,000 of income and would be left with $7,500. But if you put the money in the 401(k), the entire $10,000 of income goes into the plan. So by reducing your taxes, you have an extra $2,500 a year available for savings. So which way makes more sense: save $10,000 in a 401(k) and get a tax cut, or save $10,000 outside of a 401(k) and pay extra taxes? Clearly, maximizing your 401(k) is the most effective way to reach your savings goals.

Moreover, as long as the money remains in the 401(k), it

continues to grow *tax deferred.* This means you do not pay any taxes on interest, dividends, or capital gains on your investments within the 401(k). The money is not taxed until you begin to take distributions in retirement, and then only the money that comes out of the plan is taxed. The rest continues to grow tax-deferred. This is a very powerful wealth-building tool.

If you don't save your money in a 401(k), not only does it cost you more in taxes initially, but each year you have to pay tax on your interest, dividends, and any capital gains on your investments. A rough estimate is that you would probably be paying about 15% a year in taxes on those investment returns. Those taxes just reduce your capital every year and make it harder to move from laborer to capitalist.

> Example: Assume you contribute $10,000 to your 401(k) and earn 7.5% a year for 25 years. At the end of that period, your $10,000 would be worth $60,983. Compare that to investing $10,000 outside of the 401(k). Since you don't get the income tax deduction, it costs you $2,500 in taxes (assuming a 25% tax rate), which means you only have $7,500 to invest. Assume that grows at 7.5% per year, but assume you must pay taxes of 15% per year on that growth. The taxes reduce your return to 6.38%. After 25 years, you would only have $35,201. This is only 58% of what you would have if you had used your 401(k). Ouch.

## Icing on the Cake

The icing on the 401(k) cake is the employer contribution. Many employers make either matching or fixed contributions to their employees' 401(k) accounts. A matching contribution is one where the employer makes a contribution to your account only if you also make one—thus, they match your contribution. If you have a matching formula, it is critical that you contribute to get the matching funds. The most common match is about 3% of pay. This means if you put in at least 3%, then the employer puts in 3%.

Some companies use a fixed contribution. This means your employer puts money into your 401(k) regardless of whether you make a contribution. The most common fixed contribution is also 3%, which means the employer puts in 3% for all employees, whether they contribute to their savings or not. That's a pretty good deal.

### FOR MONEY WONKS

In the United States we have a graduated income tax system. This means the higher your income goes, the higher your tax rate is. When you contribute money to a 401(k) plan, these funds come from the part of your income that is subject to your highest income tax rate. For example, assume you make $100,000 and want to contribute $10,000 to your 401(k) plan. The $10,000 comes off the top; it is the income you earn between $90,000 and $100,000. This income is currently subject to a 25% federal income tax rate, which is the highest rate you are paying at $100,000 (assuming you file a joint return with your spouse). No matter what level of income you make, the 401(k) money comes from your highest tax bracket. On your tax form, it is deducted from the top of your wages, which is very helpful.

Consequently, when you use a Traditional 401(k) plan you are getting the biggest tax savings you can because your highest taxed dollars are going into the plan. But when you retire and take money out of your plan, that income will be subject to the graduated income tax system (assuming we still have the same tax structure that we have had for the last 100 years). Because the system is graduated, it is likely that some of your income will be taxed at the lower rates, which today would be 10% and 15%. Basically, you changed your tax rate on some of that money from 25% to less than 15%. Not bad.

The employer contribution is money that you get to keep and is a part of your pay, once it is "vested." Being "vested" means that you are entitled to keep the employer matching funds if you leave the company. Many companies immediately vest their contributions for employee 401(k) plans, but vesting schedules can last as long as five years, which means you gain ownership of 20% of the funds per year. Check with your human resources department to determine what your vesting schedule is for your 401(k) plan. In general, it doesn't take long to vest in your employer contributions.

The employer contribution is incredibly helpful for two reasons. First, if you are having trouble hitting your Savings Ratio, the employer contribution can be used to get you there. This means less stress on the family budget. Second, if you are able to hit your Savings Ratio, the match is extra capital that accelerates your Capital to Income Ratio. Either way, this is a big deal and you need to take full advantage of it.

The following chart summarizes the total positive effect that using a tax-deductible savings plan with an employer match can have on your family finances. I use a household income of $100,000, and assume a 25% income tax rate on the amount you are saving. The chart compares saving outside of a 401(k) with saving inside a 401(k). There are three 401(k) examples: saving 12% on your own without a 401(k), saving 12% of pay and using the employer match to boost you to 15%, and saving 9% and using the employer match to help you get to the base goal of 12%. Either way, the 401(k) wins:

|  | No 401(k) | 401(k) Using Match in Addition to 12% | 401(k) Using Match to Get to 12% |
|---|---|---|---|
| Salary | $100,000 | $100,000 | $100,000 |
| Savings | $12,000 | $12,000 | $9,000 |
| Match | $0 | $3,000 | $3,000 |

|  | No 401(k) | 401(k) Using Match in Addition to 12% | 401(k) Using Match to Get to 12% |
|---|---|---|---|
| Taxes on Savings at 25% | $3,000 | $0 | $0 |
| Total Savings | **$9,000** | **$15,000** | **$12,000** |

As you can see, if you save 12% on your own without a 401(k), the taxes consume a big part of your savings and you are only left with $9,000. Compare that to saving 12% in the plan and using the employer match. In that case, you saved the same $12,000, but, because you took advantage of the tax savings and match, you added $15,000 into your retirement plan. Basically, you are adding 66% more in capital by using the 401(k) and the match.

Even if you can't save the full 12%, you will get a much better result if you save 9% within the 401(k) plan and use the 3% match to get you to 12%. In the last column, you saved $9,000, but got $12,000. This is better than the first option, where you saved $12,000, but only wound up with $9,000.

What this chart is meant to illustrate is that the tax savings and employer match are critical to helping you build more capital. The best approach is to maximize your 401(k) contribution and use the match to boost your total savings each year. With the standard match being about 3%, you can drive your savings rate up to 15% before age 45 and 18% thereafter. But if you can't do that (and many people can't, especially if the kids are still home), then you should at least use the employer match to get you to 12% of pay. If you are using the employer match to get to 12%, once the kids are a little older or there is some more room in the budget, you should ramp up your savings to 15% and use the match to put you at 18%.

No matter how you do it, make sure you use the match to at least get to 12%. And if you can do more, then do more.

## Individual Retirement Account (IRA)

If you don't have a 401(k) plan, or your savings goal exceeds what you can put into a 401(k), then the next place you should look to save is an IRA. IRAs are tax-deferred retirement accounts that can be set up by individuals, as opposed to 401(k)s, which can only be set up by businesses. If you put money in an IRA, you get a tax deduction for the contribution just as you do when you put money in a 401(k). Also, the funds must remain in the IRA until at least age 59½, at which point you can take distributions for retirement. If you take a distribution before 59½, you must pay the 10% penalty tax, on top of the regular income taxes.

Now for the bad part. The contribution limits on IRAs are very low in comparison to 401(k)s. Plus, there is no employer match in an IRA. But if you don't have a 401(k) and have no other options, you can at least get some tax-deferred benefit from saving some of your capital in an IRA.

The rules for IRA contributions are straightforward if you don't have a 401(k) or any other sort of employee retirement plan, such as a profit-sharing plan. If you are under age 50, the contribution limits are $5,000 per person, starting in 2009. If you are age 50 or over, it is $6,000 per person. If you have no 401(k) plan and neither you nor your spouse are otherwise covered by an employee pension of any sort, then you should use your IRA (but always check with your accountant first).

IRAs get tricky if you or your spouse is covered by a 401(k) or another employee retirement plan. In their ever-generous spirit, the IRS does not want you using two tax deductible accounts to save money. When you have a 401(k) or you are covered by any sort of an employee retirement plan, your ability to also use an IRA is very limited. This is how it works, in a nutshell:

- In general, in 2010, if you are single and have a household income below $66,000, or if you are married with a household income below $109,000, then you may be able to put some money in an IRA, in addition to your 401(k).
- Also, if your spouse does not work, but you work and are covered by a 401(k) or other pension plan, your nonworking spouse may be able to fund an IRA if you have a household income below $177,000.

The rules are technical and the income limits change, so check with your accountant before funding any type of IRA.

> Congress could simplify all of this by just equalizing the 401(k) and IRA contribution limits and allowing employers to match IRA contributions. But that doesn't seem to be in the cards anytime soon. So for most people, the 401(k) is the best option.

## Roth Versus Regular

The 401(k) and IRA plans I've talked about so far are called Traditional plans. These were the first types of retirement plans available for companies and individuals. A few years ago, Congress passed new legislation for what are called Roth 401(k) and Roth IRA plans. The differences have to do with the way in which the accounts are taxed. Regardless of which one you use, they are both far superior to saving money outside of a 401(k) or IRA plan.

The Traditional 401(k) or IRA gives you a tax deduction for the amount you contribute each year. This saves you money at the time of the contribution, which makes it easier to reach your savings goal. Once the money is in the 401(k) or IRA, it grows tax-deferred in the account, so you don't pay any income or other taxes on your interest, dividends, or capital gains that you earn within the account. As the funds are distributed, you pay income taxes only on the amount that is distributed.

Roth accounts work in the exact opposite way. You don't get any income tax deduction on your contributions into a Roth 401(k) or IRA. This makes it harder to reach your savings goal because you have to pay taxes before you can contribute that money to your account. However, the money grows *tax-free* thereafter. You never pay tax on the money again, even when you take distributions.

> Example: Assume you have $12,000 available in your budget to contribute to your Roth 401(k). Because you don't get a deduction, you pay current income taxes on those funds, which would cost about $3,000, assuming you are in the 25% income tax bracket. Now you are left with $9,000 to save. Let's assume that that money grows to be worth $75,000 at retirement, and that you take out $25,000 as a distribution in your first year. That money is not subject to income tax. In fact, no matter how large the account grows, the money you take out is not subject to any further income tax. There are no income limits for Roth 401(k) contributions.

While Roth 401(k) contributions are not subject to income limits, Roth IRAs are. For 2009, you generally cannot contribute any funds to a Roth IRA if you are single and make more than $120,000 or married and earn more than $176,000. Again, the rules are technical so check with your tax advisor before funding any IRA.

## Which One?

So which should you choose: Roth or Traditional? Before I answer that question, we have to go through a simple, painless math exercise. Add the following numbers together:

$$2 + 3 + 4 = 9$$

Now change the order of the numbers and add them again:

$$4 + 2 + 3 = 9$$

When adding numbers, you get the same result regardless of the order of the numbers. Now multiply the following numbers:

$$2 \times 3 \times 4 = 24$$

Now change the order of the numbers and multiply them again:

$$4 \times 2 \times 3 = 24$$

When multiplying, just like when adding, the order of the numbers doesn't matter. You get the same result. This means that, if your tax rate is the same while working as it is when you're retired, it doesn't matter which account you use. You will end up with the exact same result, regardless of whether you pay taxes first or last. The tax rate is just a number that gets multiplied against your account value, and it doesn't matter when you multiply it—when you earn the money, or when you withdraw it to fund your retirement.

Let's go back to our example couple, Kevin and Amber:

Example: Let's say Kevin is 45 years old, makes $100,000, and can afford to dedicate $15,000 a year of his salary to savings. The money will be invested for 20 years and will earn 7.5% per year. We'll also assume his income tax rate is 25% while working and will be 25% in retirement. If Kevin uses a Traditional 401(k), he contributes the entire $15,000 into the plan. It grows for 20 years at 7.5% and is worth $63,717 when he retires. If he takes all the money out that year to pay expenses and pays a 25% tax on it, after paying the tax of $15,929, he and his wife are left with $47,788 to spend.

Instead, Kevin and Amber choose a Roth IRA. Now Kevin must pay tax on the $15,000 he saves per year. At a 25% tax rate, he only has $11,250 left to put in the plan. This $11,250 grows tax-free for 20 years at 7.5%. When Kevin is age 65, it is worth $47,788. At retirement, he takes all the money out and pays no tax. Voilà. In both cases, you end up with $47,788.

So what's the point in having Roth and Traditional IRAs at all? Why the difference if there's no advantage? Well, assuming your tax rate is the same pre- and postretirement, it won't matter if you use a Traditional or a Roth plan. The potential advantage comes if you feel you will have a different postretirement tax rate than you do today. Basically, if you think you will be in a lower income-tax bracket in retirement, the Traditional plan works better; if you think you will be in a higher income-tax bracket in retirement, the Roth works better. But the reality is that most of us can't be sure whether we will be in a higher or lower tax bracket once we retire. There are two reasons for this.

First, our graduated income tax system means our income is subject to multiple tax rates each year. In 2010, if you make $100,000 and file a joint return, the income below $16,750 is taxed at 10%, the income between $16,750 and $68,000 is taxed at 15%, and then the rest is taxed at 25%. The same will most likely be true when you take funds out of your plan in retirement. Some money will be taxed in the lower brackets and some in the higher brackets. Second, predicting future tax rates is basically about trying to predict who will have political power. That's a fool's game.

Thus, a prudent approach is to use both the Traditional and the Roth plans. If your 401(k) plan offers a Roth feature, you can put all or a part of your money into the Roth plan. You could decide to put 50% into the Traditional Plan and 50% into the Roth. That way you get a deduction on half the money, but get tax-free growth on the other half. The funds all go into the same place within your retirement plan, but for accounting purposes the retirement plan administrator will keep track of the two sources of contributions. When you retire, you know which money you need to pay tax on and which money you don't.

If your tax rate turns out to be lower in retirement, then you got the better deal on the Traditional plan. If your tax rate turns out to be higher, then you scored with the Roth. Splitting the allocation is probably the most prudent way to go, unless you are confident you know what your tax rate will be in retirement. If you are, I may have a job for you.

| | |
|---|---|
| *Lower Tax Rate in Retirement* | *Traditional Plan Wins* |
| *Higher Tax Rate in Retirement* | *Roth Plan Wins* |
| *Not Sure* | *Split It* |

### FOR MONEY WONKS

Let's say tax rates went up by the time you retired and the 25% rate went to 30%. If you have both a Traditional plan and a Roth plan, you have some good options. You can take distributions from your Traditional plan until you fill up the lower tax brackets at 10% and 15%. Again, this is a great

deal for you because you avoided paying 25% when you were
working and now that money is only being taxed at 10% and
15%. Then, when you get to the 30% bracket, you switch to
taking distributions from your Roth account.

The money that went into the Roth side of the 401(k)
was money you paid 25% tax on when you were working.
Remember, you didn't get a deduction for those funds when
you contributed to the plan. But now because rates went up,
you are able to take that money out and avoid paying the 30%
tax rate that would have otherwise applied. Thus you paid
25% in taxes while working and avoided a 30% tax in
retirement, which gives you a 5% advantage. That's called
working both sides of Wall Street.

## Taxable Accounts

If your annual savings goal exceeds what you can contribute to your
401(k) or IRA, you will need to open a taxable investment account.
A taxable investment account is basically an account that you open
at a brokerage firm through which you can invest in mutual funds,
stocks, and bonds. The main difference between these accounts and
a 401(k) or IRA is the tax treatment. You do not receive any sort
of tax deduction for money contributed to a taxable investment
account nor do you receive any tax-deferred or tax-free growth.

In a taxable account, you pay tax on your interest, dividends, and
any capital gains each year. This makes it harder to accumulate capital because the taxes are always skimming a portion of your assets
each year and giving them to Uncle Sam. The best you can do is
implement tax-efficient investment strategies. You will still pay tax,
but buy limiting the number of transactions you do and using tax
sensitive investment holdings, you can reduce your tax rate, which
of course helps you retain more capital.

# 5

# The Debt Ratios

Debt is the second-most important of the four major areas of personal finance to manage effectively. The reason is that many of us will need to carry some debt when we are younger (unless you are lucky enough to inherit a sizable amount of money). Keeping your debt to a manageable level is critical to creating cash flow for your savings. If your debt load is too high, there won't be any money available to save, which means you have no chance of progressing from laborer to capitalist.

Let's ask the Unifying Question:

"Will debt help move me from being a laborer to a capitalist?"

The short answer is yes. Some debt can help you move from laborer to capitalist. The long answer is, it depends. Carrying too much of the wrong kind of debt will restrict your ability to make that transition. The key is to understand which type of debt can help and which can hurt. In this chapter, I'm going to change the way you see debt, including that most sacred of all debts, the home mortgage.

## Balancing Your Debt

There are two categories of debt: Income-Producing and Income-Reducing. Income-Producing Debt includes *reasonable* housing, education, and transportation debt. These three types of debt can facilitate your ability to earn more income and transform you from a laborer to a capitalist. Income-Reducing Debt includes all credit card debt and any form of consumer debt. This type of debt does nothing to help you create more income. It basically causes you to pay more for the goods and services you are buying and reduces your future income. The only people it helps are the ones at the credit card companies.

Income-Reducing Debt also includes *excessive* housing, education, and transportation debt. You can turn Income-Producing Debt into Income-Reducing Debt if you take on too much of it. It's important to remember that debt by itself is neither good nor evil. If used properly, debt can help you build capital. If used foolishly, it can destroy your capital.

In your transition from laborer to capitalist, you will be on both sides of the debt equation. When you are younger and don't have much capital, you will be a borrower. You will borrow money to help you acquire the assets that will help you build your capital. As you age and accumulate capital, you will become a lender. You will lend your capital to companies or to our government as a part of your investment plan.

Thus, having a healthy debt market is important to all of us. We need people to be willing to lend to us when we don't have enough capital, and we need to be willing to lend to others when we have excess capital. But the debt markets only work if the borrowers have the ability to pay back the loans. The key to healthy debt is to keep it in proper proportion to the borrower's income. The reason we have had so much trouble with debt lately and so many problems with the U.S. economy is because debt has not been kept in proportion to people's incomes. People have borrowed too much money to buy homes, cars, education, and vacations. Ultimately, the debt load buries the borrower. When the borrower defaults, both the borrower and the lender lose. In this case, not only individual borrowers but huge banks and lenders have taken huge losses and the lending market has been crippled.

When you take on debt, the debt load must be small enough so that you can meet your Savings Ratio each year in addition to paying for all of the other obligations and expenses you will have in your life. The Debt Ratios in this chapter are designed to leave enough room in your budget to meet the Savings Ratio. Of course, all things being equal, the less debt you incur in general, the better. The ratios are designed to illustrate the maximum debt that you could consider incurring. If you are below the ratios, that's a good thing.

I'm going to talk about the four main kinds of debt that most people will take on in their lives: housing, education, transportation, and consumer debt. For housing and education debt, I will provide you with ratios on the debt and ways to reduce that debt as you age. For transportation debt, we will talk about how to take on only what you need to facilitate earning a living. At the end, I'll say a few words about the problems with consumer debt and how you should avoid it like the plague. First, let's completely upend how you think about that mortgage you're paying.

## Housing Debt

Let's start with the Unifying Question:

> Will borrowing money to buy a house help move
> me from being a laborer to a capitalist?

Yes, if the borrowing is done in proportion to your income. You need a place to live. A home allows you to create a place of safety, security, and comfort, and facilitates your ability to work each day. Thus, a home provides a foundation for generating income. That really, truly is the primary reason, from a capitalist standpoint, to own a home. It's not that you get a mortgage tax deduction. And it's certainly not the emotional satisfaction that comes with owning a part of the American Dream. Those are important things, but not from the perspective of moving from laborer to capitalist. Remember, the purpose of my ratios is to *take the emotion out* of that journey.

While a home facilitates your ability to work, the other economic return you will get from your house comes after you fully pay off your mortgage. At that point, you have a free place to live with no mortgage or rental costs, just property taxes and maintenance. Having a free place to live reduces your expenses in retirement. You don't have to dedicate the earnings from your capital to paying your mortgage or rent. It allows all of the earnings on your investments to be directed toward other lifestyle expenses and needs. Thus, paying off your house increases your retirement income, and owning a home helps move you from laborer to capitalist.

Remember, your primary residence does not provide any actual income to you in your retirement years. It provides what is called "deemed income." Deemed income is the investment income you get to keep in retirement because you don't have to use that income to pay a mortgage or rent.

Now, some may insist that mortgage debt can help produce income later—what about rental properties? A rental property is an investment and does not fall under the category of your primary residence. If you have true rental property (meaning property that is fully rented either to commercial or residential tenants), the equity in the property would be considered part of your retirement savings. For purposes of *Your Money Ratios*, the Mortgage to Income Ratio refers your primary residence.

The basic rule is this: the mortgage on your home must be kept in proportion to your wages. Your housing debt should not restrict your ability to meet your Savings Ratio, which is 12% of pay prior to age 45 and 15% thereafter. If your mortgage payment is too high, then the house will actually inhibit your ability to move from laborer to capitalist. You might find that you reach age 65 with a big house but no financial assets to generate income to pay your living expenses or maintain the house. That's called being "house rich but cash poor."

As a prudent capitalist, you should consider buying a modest house based on your income. A smaller house means a smaller mortgage, which means more money to contribute toward your capital. Below is a chart of the maximum recommended Mortgage to Income Ratio starting at age 30. As you can see, the Mortgage Ratio declines with age. Why? Because it is important to be debt-free once you retire.

## MORTGAGE TO INCOME RATIO

| Age | Mortgage to Income Ratio |
|-----|--------------------------|
| 25  | 2.0 |
| 30  | 2.0 |
| 35  | 1.9 |
| 40  | 1.8 |
| 45  | 1.7 |
| 50  | 1.5 |
| 55  | 1.2 |
| 60  | 0.7 |
| 65  | 0.0 |

You use the Mortgage to Income Ratio the same way you used the Capital to Income Ratio. Take your income at a certain age, multiply it by the corresponding ratio, and this is the maximum mortgage debt you should be carrying. Let's assume you are 40 years old and make $100,000. Your mortgage debt should be no more than 1.8 times your income, or about $180,000. That doesn't mean you can only afford a house worth $180,000; it does mean you should not take on a debt of more than that amount. So if you want more house, you'd better be ready to save for a bigger down payment.

The maximum mortgage debt that I recommend is 2.0 times pay when you are in your early 30s. At 2.0 times pay, assuming an interest rate of about 6.5% on a 30-year mortgage, the monthly payments will consume approximately 15% of your wages. Now remember that you will also be saving 12% to 15%. Then you owe income and employment taxes on all your wages, which for most people will be at least another 20% of pay. What is left is what you can spend on running

## MONEY FOR THE HOUSE

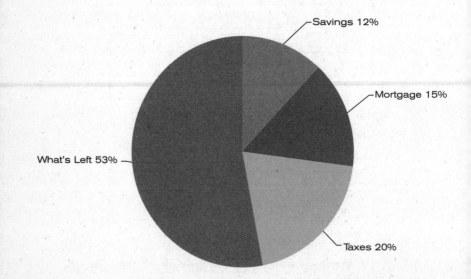

the household, buying groceries, taking care of the kids, paying for health insurance, and so on. When you subtract the big-ticket items, this leaves you with about 53% of your pay to run the house. If your mortgage costs eat up a bigger piece of the household budget, it is unlikely that you will have enough available for savings.

That "what's left" has to pay for everything from auto insurance to school tuition to utility bills to the car payment, and it doesn't stretch very far. There isn't much money left even with a mortgage that only consumes 15% of pay. Living *beneath* your means when it comes to your mortgage is not only wise, it's mandatory.

## It's Not the Payment, It's the Percentage

The housing crisis of 2008 and 2009 was a grim confirmation of the Mortgage to Income Ratio. People have borrowed too much money to buy their homes. The mortgage costs are eating up a huge percentage of their budgets, leaving them with little or no funds to pay other living expenses. Unfortunately, banks and other mortgage lenders were approving people for loans that they could not afford. It is important to understand that a bank or a mortgage broker is not a great place to get guidance regarding a loan. Why? Because bankers and brokers don't care if you have the ability to build capital for retirement. They care about making loans and generating fees on those loans. In recent years, lenders were approving mortgages that were eating up as much as 35% of the borrower's incomes—and if they couldn't manage that, borrowers were getting into dangerous subprime, adjustable-rate, and reverse-amortization loans that deferred the big debt until later—but like a great white shark, debt is always out there, waiting. Let's bring the Capital to Income Ratio, Savings Ratio, and Mortgage to Income Ratio together:

| Age 65 & 80% Income Replacement | | | |
|---|---|---|---|
| Age | Capital to Income Ratio | Savings Ratio | Mortgage to Income Ratio |
| 25 | 0.1 | 12% | 2.0 |
| 30 | 0.6 | 12% | 2.0 |
| 35 | 1.4 | 12% | 1.9 |
| 40 | 2.4 | 12% | 1.8 |
| 45 | 3.7 | 15% | 1.7 |
| 50 | 5.2 | 15% | 1.5 |
| 55 | 7.1 | 15% | 1.2 |
| 60 | 9.4 | 15% | 0.7 |
| 65 | 12.0 | 15% | 0.0 |

Now you can see a long-term plan for building capital and reducing debt. You need to make progress on each front throughout your working career. As you systematically work your way forward through each aspect of the ratios, you will gradually be making progress toward the final result: a secure retirement.

On the other hand, if you exceed the Mortgage to Income Ratio, you are likely to find it difficult to meet the Savings Ratio, which means you will have difficulty meeting your Capital to Income Ratio. Each of the ratios is tied to the others and you need to be managing them in concert to make steady progress from laborer to capitalist.

The Mortgage to Income Ratio is small enough to allow you to save 12% early in your career and 15% later in your career. One important thing to remember about a traditional mortgage is that, on an inflation-adjusted basis, the payments are going down each year as your income slowly rises with inflation. For instance, assume you have a monthly mortgage payment of $1,000 when you are age 40. If you used a 30-year fixed mortgage it will still be $1,000 at age 60. But, your income will have likely almost doubled in that period, if it simply grows with the inflation rate of about 3% a year. This means it is becoming easier and easier to pay your mortgage.

Consequently, your mortgage payment should fall as a percentage of your monthly pay as you age. As the mortgage falls as a percentage of your pay, you can jump your savings rate up to 15% in your mid 40s and thereafter. This will help you accelerate your capital accumulation during your peak earnings years and help combat the risk that the financial markets may not provide the returns you were anticipating. Also, if you have kids, they will probably be hitting college sometime in your mid 40s to early 50s. Thus, it would be good planning to have some extra cash flow if you plan on assisting them.

If you fall behind in your savings goals early in your working career, it will be very hard to catch up. The reason is time. As your time horizon shortens, you have to save double or triple the amount you would have needed if you had just started earlier. And, often you don't have the money to save double or triple the amount. The power of compounding means it is very important to start saving at least 12% of pay by age 30. Thus, your mortgage has to be small enough to allow you to do this. If not, you will find that you have made the path from laborer to capitalist a lot harder than it has to be, and in fact may never get there.

Example: If you save 12% a year starting at age 25, then you should be making steady progress toward accumulating 12 times pay by age 65. But if you only save 5% a year from ages 25 to 40, how much harder will it be from ages 41 to 65? Your savings rate must increase to an estimated 25% of pay for every year thereafter to catch up. Missing a little bit of savings in the first 10 years almost doubles your savings burden for the next 25 years. The problem is that you may not be able to save 25% of pay for 25 years.

In the early 1970s, the savings rate in America was about 11%, and the average person bought a house that cost about 2.1 times their pay. This is right in line with the ratios I recommend. But over the last 30 years, people have begun to pay more and more for their houses. At the height of the real estate boom, the average house cost about 3.9 times pay. Guess what has happened to the savings rate along the way? It went to zero. The average American was not saving any money. Why? Because at debt of about 4 times pay, the mortgage alone will consume about 30% of your total income. Since housing costs went from about 15% of pay to 30% of pay, guess where people got that extra 15% to spend on housing? They simply stopped saving.

To stay on the path from laborer to capitalist, you need to keep your mortgage debt below about two times pay and get the debt paid off before you retire. This will provide you with enough room in your budget to save 12% of your pay prior to age 45 and 15% from age 45 on. Better yet, when you get it paid off, you will have a rent-free place to live in retirement. That is as simple as it gets.

## Houses Aren't Retirement Plans

Don't make the mistake of thinking that your house can serve as both a home and a retirement plan. Remember, your goal at retirement is to accumulate financial assets that produce income to replace your wages. Your house does not produce actual income because you are living in it (as opposed to renting it to someone else). A house will facilitate your ability to earn an income and retire, but it is not an investment in the same way that your 401(k) is.

Over the last 20 years, people began to believe that real estate values increase at 8% to 10% a year or more. If this went on forever, a house might make a good retirement investment. But the increase in housing prices over the last decade is an anomaly; over the long term, most people won't make any money on their homes. There is a basic relationship between wage growth and housing costs that you can't escape. Over the long term, residential real estate values won't go up by much more than the average wage growth in a region. If they do go up by more than wage growth, then eventually no one could buy a home. The mortgage would consume all of the average family's income. This did occur during the real estate bubble of 2004–2007, but the correction has been ferocious.

Example: Assume the average homeowner in a region makes $100,000, and the average home in the region costs $400,000. Wages tend to grow a little faster than the rate of inflation over the long term. If inflation runs at 3%, then wages might grow 4.0% per year. That keeps the price of housing manageable for a good portion of the population. Now consider what happens after 30 years if wages grow at 4.0% but the cost of housing goes up 10% a year. After 30 years, the average wage in a region would go from $100,000 to about $324,000. But the cost of the average home would have gone to about $7,000,000. Assuming you put down 10% for the home, a $6,300,000 mortgage at 6.25% interest would cost $465,000 per year. If you are only making $324,000, it is going to be hard to carry a $465,000 annual mortgage expense.

You might be surprised to learn that over the last 50 years, home values in the United States have increased by only about 3% to 4% a year, even considering the big increases we had between 2000 and 2007. Inflation and wages have also gone up by about 3% to 4% a year over the same time frame. As you can see, the relationships hold pretty steady if you understand the history of these markets.

If only the people at Fannie Mae and Freddie Mac had run these numbers, they would have seen that the real estate market was bound to collapse. Now the market is correcting for the excesses. Housing prices are falling and homes are becoming more affordable because the debt load for many families is unsustainable. The human cost is that millions are in foreclosure and bankruptcy. I don't know where this process will end. If the government makes it easy for people to continue to leverage their futures, and if most homeowners decide to put all their capital into their homes instead of into building retirement assets, we may end up with the same problems that got us into this mess the first time.

The other thing about houses is that they cost money to manage. You have to insure your house, heat it, cool it, maintain it, pay taxes on it . . . the list goes on. On average, you could expect to spend about 3% to 4% of the cost of your house on repairs, maintenance, and taxes each year. Then you have a mortgage, which is probably costing you at least 6% a year. Consequently, to make money on residential real estate, your house has to appreciate at a rate greater than the 6% mortgage and 3% to 4% maintenance costs each year. That means your house has to appreciate 8% to 10% a year. In most markets, that's just not going to happen consistently.

My proof of this theory is Newport, Rhode Island. In Newport, there is a row of huge mansions on the shoreline that were built by some of America's richest families, such as the Vanderbilts. Today, nobody lives in these houses, because the people who built them couldn't afford to maintain them. Today, these homes have mostly been turned into tourist attractions where people throw a few bucks into the kitty to view what used to be a nice house. If the Vanderbilts couldn't maintain a big house, I don't think most of us have a chance of doing so either.

## Pay Off the House

You might be thinking, "Wow, Charlie, way to be a wet blanket. Maybe I should forget about buying a house in the first place." No, buying is still a good deal, because you need a place to live and you will either rent or buy. If you buy, the true value comes when you finally get the house paid off and have a free place to live. This facilitates your ability to retire and live off the return on your capital. With any luck, you have begun to realize that, all things being equal, a smaller, less expensive house will help you progress from laborer to capitalist faster.

Take the house off the table as a retirement asset and focus on paying it off by the time you retire. This gives you a rent-free place to live and allows you to dedicate more of your cash flow to doing the things you enjoy. Do you really need to pay it off? Yes. Having no debt substantially increases the odds that you will be able to live off the income from your capital for 25 or 30 years.

If you carry a mortgage into retirement, the amount of that mortgage reduces the capital you have available to produce income for your lifestyle in retirement. So if you have a Capital to Income Ratio of 12, but still carry a mortgage, you don't really have a Capital to Income Ratio of 12 because part of that capital has to be dedicated to paying the mortgage.

Example: If you remember our discussion about retirement income, you can anticipate distributing about 5% of your capital each year for retirement income. Now assume you enter your retirement years with a $300,000 mortgage at 6.5%. The monthly payments on that mortgage are about $1,900, or $22,800 per year. If you have $1.2 million in retirement capital and are getting a $60,000 distribution plus $20,000 a year from Social Security, then you have $80,000 a year to live on. But after paying your mortgage, you only have $57,200. You've reduced your annual income by nearly 30%.

There is one other aspect of retirement that makes paying off the mortgage critical. Remember, in retirement, you are living off the returns on your capital. The 5% distribution figure we discussed is an estimate and is certainly not guaranteed in any given year or economic cycle. At times, you may need to take less to get through a difficult period. When the economy gets bad, as it does every so many years, the returns in the financial markets fall. Stock prices and interest rates decline. As the returns fall, the income you can generate from your capital falls. But your debt payments don't change. This means that if you carry debt, and your investment income falls, you will have to dedicate a larger percentage of whatever income you can generate toward paying your debts.

If your reduced income cannot cover your debt payments and basic living expenses, then you need to sell capital to cover the expenses. Because the market is bad, you will be selling capital at a depressed price, and you can burn through a huge percentage of your life's savings in a few years. Even if the economy recovers, with less capital, you may not be able to generate enough income to support yourself for the rest of your retirement.

Remember the discussion about dropping your distribution rate from 5% to 4%? The Capital to Income Ratio is designed to give you flexibility to make it through these cycles—as long as you don't carry any debt. If you retire with $1,200,000 of capital and a $300,000 mortgage at 6.5%, the mortgage is consuming $22,800 of your anticipated $80,000 of income each year. Now throw in a bear market when your distribution falls to 4%. Instead of $80,000 of income, you now have $68,000, but that mortgage debt is still eating up $22,800 a year. This leaves you with only $45,200 to live on, or about 57% of your goal. The debt payments reduce your flexibility to deal with changing financial markets and thus increase the odds that you may run out of money in retirement. If you want to be in a position to weather the volatility in the markets, you need to retire with no debt.

Because the financial markets are so volatile, you need to anticipate swings in your investment income. If your income falls in retirement, you adjust by scaling back your spending. You can skip a vacation, delay buying a car, go out to dinner less, etc. But you cannot change your debt payments. That is why they are so dangerous. You need to anticipate that there will be periods when your income falls in retirement, and thus you need to get your finances prepared to deal with these changes. Otherwise, you are simply hoping to get lucky, and that is not how a prudent capitalist operates. Luck is not a success strategy. Buy a modest house and pay it off before age 65. Please.

## Live Where You Can Afford

Even with the real estate market falling, homes are still very expensive on the coasts, especially in places like California and New York. But remember that there are large parts of this country where buying a home under the Mortgage to Income Ratio is very achievable, like the Midwest and South. You will need to decide if living in one of the expensive parts of the country is worth it. If you are struggling to make a mortgage payment and can't save for your retirement, then maybe it isn't. There is no law against moving to another state.

Consider how a business would approach this problem. If costs were too high in one part of the country to support the business at profitable levels, the owners of that business would move to a location that allows them to run a profitable business. This is the same for individuals. If you are a finance executive, New York may be just fine if the income from your job is high enough to allow you to comfortably live in New York. If you are a doctor, you may find you can generate the same income in Kansas City as in New York, and Kansas City costs half as much.

While I caution you against treating your house as a retirement investment and counting your equity as a part of your Capital to Income Ratio, there is one scenario where this might be appropriate. If you plan on selling your home and moving to a *less expensive* house in retirement, then you can include a portion of your equity in your retirement savings. Essentially, the difference between the proceeds from the sale of your current house and the cost of the smaller house could be counted as part of your savings.

For example, assume you own a $1 million house in California and fully pay it off by age 65. Now you retire and decide to move to Iowa and buy a $400,000 house. You could arguably consider the $600,000 difference as part of your retirement savings. That $600,000 could be added to your Capital to Income Ratio. But be realistic. If you live in a high-cost area of the country, the only way to realize any value from the sale of the house is to move to a lower-cost area. Are you really going to do this? Many people live in certain parts of the country because they enjoy the lifestyle, weather, and culture, or they have family in the region. Once you retire and have the free time to enjoy the area where you live even more, is it likely you will want to move?

Some people also believe that while they won't move to a less expensive part of the country, they will buy a less expensive house in their current community. Well, I suggest you take a look around at what you could get. Less expensive generally means the house is smaller, in a less desirable location, and needs updating. Again, be realistic with yourself. If you want to live in a less expensive house, do it now and save yourself all that money in the meantime. If you aren't willing to do it now, I doubt you will be willing to do it when you retire. Before you count any part of your home equity in your Capital to Income Ratio, make sure you are fully committed to moving to a less expensive house.

One final note on the subject of equity: the reverse mortgage. A reverse mortgage allows you to pull a certain amount of equity out of your house in retirement, but still stay in the home. Essentially, you sell your house to a bank, get a monthly income stream, but still get to live in the house. It sounds good, but in reality it is a last-ditch effort to generate income in retirement. Once you enter into a reverse mortgage, you have basically played your last card. Plus, the terms are often not that favorable and it is an expensive way to access equity in your home. Don't plan on using one of these unless you have run out of options. A reverse mortgage is a safety net and should not be considered part of your long-term plan.

## Renting: The Right Option for Some

Because housing is so expensive in certain parts of the country, many people would be better off renting for a part of their working careers. If your finances are not strong enough to allow you to buy a home under the Mortgage to Income Ratio, then rent for 10 or 15 years until you can buy a home under the ratio. You can rent a place for a lot less than you can buy one. If you think you are going to have a hard time owning a home and saving 12% to 15% of pay, it is better to build your Capital to Income Ratio Ratio and buy a home later.

Example: Assume buying a home will cost you 30% of your income, which is common in many parts of the country, and renting will cost you 20%. You would be better off renting and saving the other 10% of pay in your retirement plan. If you make $100,000 a year and saved that extra $10,000 instead of putting it into a house, by the time you retired you would have about $1,150,000 (in today' dollars), assuming you earned a 4.5% real return on your savings each year. At that point, you could go out and buy a $250,000 house for cash, which still leaves you $900,000 in retirement assets. Assuming you can take a 5% distribution from those funds, you would have $45,000 of income in retirement before Social Security. Add in the assumed $20,000 from Social Security and you are at 65%

income replacement (when we net out inflation). Compare this outcome to the one where you funnel 30% of your pay into your mortgage and have no money for savings. You will reach age 65 with a house, but no assets to pay your living expenses.

Renting requires that you set aside the emotional aspect of buying a home. People want permanence and to own something of their own, but if that doesn't make sense for you now, then it doesn't. You have to set aside the emotion and make a cold financial calculation based on what's best for you in the long term. Forget about the "owning your own home" version of the American Dream. I prefer the "retiring comfortably at 65" version. For some, that means renting.

## When to Buy

With the recent decline in housing prices, you also must rethink how a house fits into your overall financial plan. Prior to this crisis, housing prices generally didn't fall much, and it was relatively easy to sell a home. But now we have a widespread decline in housing prices, ranging from 5% to 30% in some areas. Since housing prices are a lot more volatile than previously believed, we need to approach home ownership with the same strategies we use for other volatile assets, such as the stock market. The rule of thumb is that if you need your money in less than 10 years, you shouldn't invest it in the stock market. The same theory should apply to housing.

In fact, it is more important for housing because a house is a leveraged asset, meaning that we borrow money to buy it. If the value of the house declines by just a small amount, you can lose most of your investment because the losses are magnified by the debt.

Example: Assume you buy a $300,000 house and put 20% down, or $60,000. If the house falls 10% in value, from

$300,000 to $270,000, you have lost 50% of your $60,000 investment. Thus a 10% price decline produces a 50% loss of your investment. Now consider that it also costs about 5% in commissions simply to sell your house. This means you would receive about $255,000 on the sale, and your mortgage is $240,000, which leaves you with $15,000 of the $60,000 you invested. When you net it all out, a 10% decline in price causes you to lose 75% of your $60,000 investment.

Compare this to investing $60,000 in the stock market that also declines 10% in value. Now your stocks are worth $54,000, but you can sell them in an instant and walk away. The 10% stock market decline produced a 10% loss; the 10% housing decline produced a 75% loss.

Consequently, if you think you may need to move in less than 10 years, it is probably not a good idea to lock yourself into a home. If the price declines, you don't have enough time to wait out a recovery. Because you also borrowed money to buy the house, the decline can have a much worse effect on your investment than what you might see from the stock market. In this situation, consider renting and save your money.

There's another reason to buy carefully. Because we live in a fluid economy, at times we are required to relocate to continue with our jobs. If you have a big mortgage and the real estate market declines, you may not be in a financial position to move. If you can't sell and get out from underneath the debt, the house may actually prohibit you from advancing in your career.

This is another reason why, even if you don't believe you will need to move in 10 years, owning a smaller home is more advantageous. If you must move to continue with your employment, it is easier to sell a smaller home. Plus, if the home is less expensive, and you end up losing some money, your losses will be more manageable.

Otherwise, the house may actually restrict your ability to move from laborer to capitalist.

## Mortgage Options: Keep It Simple

What type of mortgage should you get? This is not as important as how much debt you should take on. But I want to address it because so many people make mistakes in this area.

First rule: keep your debt low by following the Mortgage to Income Ratio. Then think about the cheapest money you can get to finance the house. Most people approach it from the opposite viewpoint. They use the structure of the mortgage loan to help them buy a bigger house. Over the last few years, we have seen interest-only, adjustable-rate, and negative-amortization loans come on the market. These things are a disaster for most people. The recent financial crisis only proves this point. These types of loans go way beyond the fundamentals of what you need, and have been used to get people to borrow more than they can afford. There can be places for these other exotic loans, but they are sophisticated financing vehicles and are generally only appropriate (if at all) for people with significant wealth.

Stick with a traditional fixed rate mortgage for 30, 20, or 15 years. The payments on a 30-year will be the lowest because you have more time to pay back the debt. For most people, this makes the most sense. It provides you with the lowest payment, but still gets the house paid off by the time you intend to retire. The lower payment will help you have more room for savings and hitting your 12% goal early in your working career.

Although taking out a 30-year mortgage at age 40 would have you paying until age 70, you can always put yourself on a payment plan to pay it down in 25 years. Traditional fixed rate mortgages allow you to pay extra principal each month and shorten the time of the loan. Just make sure there is no prepayment penalty.

> Example: Assume you borrow $200,000 at 6.5% at age 40, using a 30-year mortgage. The payment is $1,264 a month, and you would be paying until age 70. To get the mortgage paid off by 65, just ask the mortgage company to tell you how much you need to pay to get it paid off in 25 years. The payment would be $1,350 per month. All you have to do is add another $86 to your monthly mortgage payment and you will be done by 65.

However, if you are 50 or older and buying a new home, don't get a 30-year mortgage. You need a 15-year mortgage and to get it paid off by age 65. If you can't afford the 15-year mortgage, then you are probably borrowing too much at that age.

The reason a fixed rate loan is your best deal is because you get to lock in a specific interest rate for the term of the loan. If rates are low when you get the loan, good. They cannot go up and you will get a good deal. If rates are high when you get your mortgage, there is not much you can do about it at that time. You will get an interest rate that is competitive for the current cost of money. But, if rates fall in the future, you can refinance to the lower rate. So, there really is no reason not to use a fixed rate mortgage, because it is heads you win and tails you win.

So if you're young, should you go for a 15-year or 30-year mortgage? Technically, you will come out the same, but practically, a 30-year mortgage is easier, because it provides you with extra funds to allocate toward your savings. Assume you have a 30-year 6.5% mortgage for a $200,000 loan. This costs $1,264 a month. A 15-year mortgage would carry a little lower rate, say 6.25%, and would cost $1,714 a month. The difference is about $450 a month, or $5,400 a year. If you take that extra $5,400 and put it in your retirement plan, that will help you get to your 12% savings goal.

You could argue that if you pay off your house in 15 years, the money you were using to pay your mortgage could then go into your retirement savings. But things happen. Kids are born, people get sick, and so on. You may not be able to save that money later on, so it's generally better to save more today and carry a mortgage for a longer period. If paying for 30 years really bothers you, try making one extra payment per year, just applied to principal. Do this every year and you'll pay off your 30-year mortgage in about 24 years.

From an investment standpoint, there is an important technical argument for using the 30-year mortgage and saving the difference in your retirement plan. The reason is that the longer you have your money in the market, the more likely the returns will come closer to the long-term market averages and outpace your interest costs on the mortgage. If you start putting the extra money in at age 35, over the next 30 years there is a good chance you will beat a 6.5% return. If you wait and try to funnel a lot of money into the markets in the last decade before retirement, you could get unlucky and hit a cycle like the last 10 years.

Stay away from interest-only loans, adjustable-rate loans, and negative-amortization loans. An interest-only loan is like renting. You are never paying down the principal, but at some point you will have to do so. It only masks the real repayment obligation. Assume you take out a $200,000 loan at 6.5% as interest-only. That means you will have a mortgage payment of $13,000 per year (6.5% of $200,000) or $1,083 per month. Not bad. But consider you are not making any progress on paying down the principal. At some point you need to pay off the house so that you have a rent-free place to live. Interest-only is just delaying the inevitable.

A negative-amortization loan is even worse. With this type of loan, you don't even have to pay the full $13,000 of interest each year. You can actually pay less. Sounds great, but that interest that you are not paying simply gets added to the principal. Assume you pay $10,000 in interest for the year, but actually owed $13,000. The extra $3,000 that you did not pay is added to your mortgage balance. Now you owe $203,000. But that is not the end of it. The interest of 6.5% is then applied to $203,000, and you owe $13,195 in interest for the next year. If you don't pay the full amount of interest again, the shortfall is added to your mortgage balance and interest is applied. You can see how this can turn into a financial death spiral.

"Negative amortization" is just finance-speak for "stupid." If you are thinking of taking out a negative-amortization loan, hold a brick about three inches above your pinky and drop it. That's a fraction of the pain you will experience with a negative-amortization loan.

Adjustable-rate loans are also dangerous because your rate can increase. For instance, if you take out your loan when rates are 5.5% and they move to 8%, the interest on your loan increases. How does that affect your payment? If you have a $200,000 loan at 5.5% and the rate goes to 8%, your payments go from $1,135 to $1,467 per month. For many people who bought too much house for their income, that's too much. "Resetting" adjustable rates are one of the reasons so many people have gone "upside down" on their mortgages and lost their homes. These types of loans are used to initially get buyers into homes they cannot otherwise afford, because the initial payment is lower. This is the wrong way to use these types of loans.

Let's keep it simple. Don't take out more than the amount indicated on my Mortgage to Income Ratio Chart. Stick with a 30-year fixed mortgage and make sure you are saving 12% to 15% of pay each year. If you are over age 50 when you buy a new house, use a 15-year mortgage to ensure that it is paid off by age 65. If you do this, you probably won't live in a McMansion, but you will enjoy the greatest luxury: peace of mind.

## Education Debt

The second-biggest debt most individuals or families will incur is for the cost of education. With in-state college tuition running $10,000 to $20,000 a year, it can cost between $40,000 and $80,000 just for a basic college degree. On top of that, you or someone in your family may want to go to graduate school, which could cost another $50,000.

Properly managing your education debt is critical to your long-term financial success. As with mortgage debt, the education debt must be kept in proportion to your wages. Education is good, but too much debt to get the education can destroy the economic benefits of the education. This applies whether the student is you or one of your kids.

Now, to the Unifying Question:

"Will education debt help me move from being a laborer to a capitalist?"

Yes. To move from laborer to capitalist status, you need a job that pays above a living wage, which provides you with excess capital to save. The more you make in that job, the more excess capital you have and the faster you can move from being a laborer to a capitalist. Education is one of the primary ingredients for getting a good job—the best jobs generally go to the best educated. If you do not get educated, then your odds of living at or just above the poverty level are high. According to the U.S. Department of Commerce, in 2006 the median annual income of a man with just a high school diploma was $37,030. With a master's degree, that median basically doubled to $75,430. If you get educated, there are far more opportunities for you to get paid a good salary. Thus, education debt can be Income-Producing Debt.

By the way, this discussion about education only applies to those who need to take on debt to finance their education. If you don't need to incur debt for your own or your kids' education, spend whatever you want. It is basically a luxury. But even if you can pay cash, analyzing the costs under basic business principles may help you spend more wisely. Also, the Debt Ratios are the maximum amount you should consider. All else being equal, the less debt the better.

## The Education Debt to Average Earnings Ratio

The general rule on education debt is to incur debt of no more than 75% of your projected average annual wages during your first 10 years of employment. This is the Education Debt to Average Earnings Ratio. Education debt should also be repaid within 10 years. At this ratio of 75% Education Debt to Average Earnings, you will roughly be using 10% of your future income to repay the loans, assuming interest rates of 6% to 8%. If you do that for 10 years, then you have given up one full year's worth of pay as the price to get educated and with luck move into a higher income bracket. Here's the ratio and payment schedule in a table:

### EDUCATION DEBT TO AVERAGE EARNINGS RATIO

| Year | Debt to Avg. Annual Earnings |
|------|------------------------------|
| 1    | 0.75                         |
| 5    | .45                          |
| 10   | 0.00                         |

Assuming you incurred these costs in your early 20s, your ratio would start at 0.75 at about age 25 and decline to zero by 35. You use this ratio the same way you use all the other ratios. Take your estimated average earnings for the next 10 years after college and multiply it by .75. This provides you with the maximum amount of debt you should consider incurring.

> Example: Assume you want to be an accountant and you esti-
> mate that over your first 10 years of work, your pay starts at
> $45,000 and tops out at $75,000. Add up your total income
> over those 10 years and you get $600,000. Divide that by 10,
> you get an average wage of $60,000 per year. Thus, you should
> take on no more than 75% of $60,000, or $45,000, as your
> education debt. If your school of choice costs more, go to a
> cheaper school.

At $45,000 of debt, assuming a 7% interest rate, your repayment obligation is about $6,300 per year. This is roughly 10% of your average annual earnings during that 10 years. When you start working after college, the repayment will be harder as your pay is lower. But you will probably have fewer expenses at that point. As the years go by and your income grows, the repayment is a little easier to make. This will be important as you will also be starting to take on other obligations, like a mortgage and family. Moreover, once you get to age 30 you have to pick up the pace on the retirement savings. That will be another 12% of your pay. If you are done with your college loans, then you will have more room for savings, a mortgage, and all the other goodies that come with being a grown-up.

What if you want to go to graduate school? Same deal. Your combined college and graduate school debt should be no more than 75% of your anticipated average annual earnings during your first 10 years of your career. Let's say you want to be a lawyer. You need to go to college and law school. You anticipate that you will start out making $70,000 a year and will progress to $100,000 over the next 10 years. When you add it all up, you get $900,000 in 10-year earnings, or $90,000 a year. Our 75% figure means you should take on no more than $67,500 of debt for your legal schooling. The repayment on that would be about $9,400 per year, or about 10% of your average annual earnings during that period.

Going to graduate school should put you in a position to get a higher-paying job. If it doesn't, you shouldn't be taking out loans to go. If it's your dream, fine. Just find a way to go without taking on more debt.

Essentially, college loans are an investment in your future wage-earning capacity. To know your potential future wages, you need to research average earnings in your anticipated field. Would you take on a loan to buy a business if you had no idea how much income the business would generate? Of course not. The loan must be in proportion to the earnings of the enterprise. This is the same with education.

## Demand Accountability

One way to do this is to pressure the schools you are thinking of attending for better data on career earnings. This is something that's seriously overdue. With tuitions skyrocketing, universities have not been required to justify their costs based on any sort of business principles. They have simply been telling people that they need to get educated and giving them the cost. The reality is that colleges have spent more money on lifestyle enhancements for the students and little time actually figuring out if the amount paid for tuition is worth it from an investment standpoint. It is not enough to say that it qualifies you for a higher-paying job. The cost must be in proportion to the anticipated pay. Demand these numbers from your college of choice.

Once you compile your research on wages in your desired field, I suggest you be conservative, unless you or your child is getting into a field that's sure to pay a healthy wage, such as medicine. Because the education system has been getting a free ride on demonstrating their economic worth, many students and parents are taking on far more debt than is justified by the earnings potential for the student. This should not be an emotional decision, but it is. We tend to approach education with a great deal of emotion. We want to give our kids the best. But the most expensive school may not be the best for you or your child. You may be better off figuring out the most cost-effective way to get the degree.

There are few schools that are worth higher debt. Certainly, some Ivy League schools may qualify, and others with specialties in certain fields that may be important to you. For instance, if you're going into engineering, the Massachusetts Institute of Technology may be worth your money. But, if you are going to incur more debt, you should be very confident that this school will open up more income opportunities for you in the future.

Even though very high wage earners, like doctors, could arguably support a little higher debt because they will likely have more discretionary income, I suggest no one go higher than 75% of average earnings unless they have enough income to pay for tuition without debt, or are a lock for big scholarships or financial aid. The reason is that even within high-paying professions, there are large discrepancies in income. For instance, pediatricians, primary care physicians, geriatricians, and researchers make much less than orthopedic surgeons and ophthalmologists. Before you take on the debt, you need to have a high level of confidence in your anticipated earnings.

This chart provides a summary of how much of your annual pay you would give up each year at various levels of debt compared to your income:

| Debt as a Percentage of Avg. Annual Pay over 10 Years | Repayment as a Percentage of Annual Pay at 7% Interest over 10 Years |
|---|---|
| 25% | 3.5% |
| 50% | 7% |
| 75% | 10% |
| 100% | 14% |
| 125% | 17% |
| 150% | 21% |

Thus, if you incur debt equal to just 25% of your anticipated average pay, the repayment costs you about 3.5% of pay for 10 years. This sounds reasonable, given that the debt probably put you in a position to make more money. At a debt rate of 50%, it costs you 7% of pay to repay the bank. Then at 75%, it is 10%. But look at the numbers for 125% and 150% of average earnings. Ugly. You are sacrificing 17% to 21% of your pay for that education. Honestly ask yourself if it is worth having that school-specific diploma when you would have gotten the same education at a school with half the tuition. Factor in income taxes of 25% to 30%, now you only have half of your income left each month before you pay the mortgage, buy food, or add anything to your 401(k) plan.

## The Reality of Rising Costs

If you have taken on debt to pay for your children's college, it is likely to inhibit your ability to build your Capital to Income Ratio. If you fall significantly behind in your late 40s and 50s because you are taking on debt for your kids' education, you may not be able to catch up. The fact is, your kids' education isn't going to help you earn more. So fund your kids' education as best you can because you love them, but if it's a choice between retirement savings and college savings, choose your 401(k).

Financially, it is better for your kids to take on the debt than for you. First, your kids have many more years available to pay back the loans. Second, if they stick with the Education Debt Ratios, they should be able to handle the repayment, and their additional career earnings throughout their working years should more than offset the costs. Third, if you have excess capital later on, you can always make gifts to your kids to help them pay off the loans. And fourth, if you follow the Money Ratios, your children will likely receive some inheritance. At that time, you are basically repaying them for any loans they had to take out for college. Thus, you have covered your own financial needs, and provided them with a nice kicker to help either pay off any loans they currently have or add to their Capital to Income Ratio.

There are many different ways to finance college, and costs are all over the board. For many people, it may make sense to go to a community or local state college for two years and then transfer to a larger university. You will still get the degree from the university and will likely have access to the same career options as if you went for the entire four years. But you will probably spend at least 30% less.

My wife, Paula, is a good example of someone who was able to obtain a Ph.D. without incurring any education debts. When she was younger, she joined the military and used the GI bill to pay for part of her college. She then got scholarships and internships to help finance her master's and Ph.D. programs. She had options to go to more expensive schools, but chose the universities that offered her a good education at a lower cost. If you ask her, I don't think she would say it has made any difference in her ability to advance in her career. But it has made it easier for us to stick to our ratios, because we didn't have to incur large debts to finance her education.

Unfortunately, the cost of education has been growing at well over two times the rate of inflation, and doesn't show any signs of slowing down. At some point, however, the cost will need to come down, just as with housing. Mathematically, we cannot pay higher and higher amounts for education if the education is not helping us earn proportionately more income. Tuition would eventually consume all of our earnings.

Although the cost of education should at some point decline, it may continue to run high for many years. I suspect the government and the higher education system will suggest that student loans be spread over longer periods of time, such as 20 and 30 years. This is the same financing trick that car companies use to lower the monthly payments, but actually increase the total cost. This would be a disaster for most people, as the debt would burden them for most of their working careers, and leave little room for them to build any other assets.

I expect that higher education will resist justifying the cost of college on economic terms, and will continue to cite vague statistics on the value of an education. Eventually, the same economic fallacy that caused the housing market to collapse—costs outpacing wage growth—will do the same to education if people continue to pile on more debt. At some point, people will realize that their career earnings are not high enough to repay the loans. Do yourself and your kids a favor and don't get into this situation. Be disciplined and apply a rational eye toward education costs.

Let's add the Education Debt to Average Earnings Ratio to our Money Ratios chart.

| The Money Ratios Age 65 & 80% Income Replacement | | | | |
|---|---|---|---|---|
| Age | Capital to Income Ratio | Savings Ratio | Mortgage to Income Ratio | Education Debt Ratio |
| 25 | 0.1 | 12% | 2.0 | .75 |
| 30 | 0.6 | 12% | 2.0 | .45 |
| 35 | 1.4 | 12% | 1.9 | 0.0 |
| 40 | 2.4 | 12% | 1.8 | X |
| 45 | 3.7 | 15% | 1.7 | X |
| 50 | 5.2 | 15% | 1.5 | X |
| 55 | 7.1 | 15% | 1.2 | X |
| 60 | 9.4 | 15% | 0.7 | X |
| 65 | 12.0 | 15% | 0.0 | X |

Take out the least amount of debt possible, given your anticipated career earnings. Plan on repaying the money within 10 years. Remember, you need to start building your Capital to Income Ratio no later than age 30. You will also be trying to buy a home during this period and probably starting a family. All of these things are expensive at a time when your earnings are modest.

## You Come First

Of course, one of the best ways to avoid debt for education is to have parents who build up a college fund. Whatever has been saved for college will reduce any debt that you may have to incur to get educated. Because college costs are increasing at a pace that exceeds inflation, it is tough to predict how much it will cost to educate a child. Still, we can run a few numbers to give you a rough assessment of what it takes to save for education. While 18 years looks like a long time, it is not when it comes to the financial markets. Thus, we have to be more conservative in our assumptions about market returns because you don't have the benefit of a 40-year investment cycle. This is a rough estimate, but given the current rate of college inflation and investment returns over a cycle shorter than 20 years, you probably shouldn't assume much more than a 2% real return on the money you are saving for your kids' education. Assuming a basic state college costs about $40,000 in today's dollars, you would need to save at least $2,000 a year starting from the day your child was born, and that assumes tuition doesn't outpace the rate of inflation. Then of course, more expensive state schools or private schools will require much more savings.

Many parents wonder if they should save for their kids' education before they save for their retirement. The answer is *absolutely not*. Save for your retirement first, the kids' education second. It is the same theory that applies to incurring debt for your kids' education. Education expenses should not impede your ability to build adequate capital for your financial security.

It sounds selfish, but it isn't. If you do well with your finances, you can always make gifts to the kids later to help them with any loans or expenses. As I pointed out before, if you have followed *Your Money Ratios*, the kids will likely receive an inheritance that will help.

The other option is to pump money into education and neglect your own financial security. The problem with this is if you don't save enough to support yourself in retirement, guess who gets the burden of doing that? Right—your kids. Trust me, they won't be happy if they have to start paying for your prescription drugs or utilities. They will have their own challenges and kids to raise. Your financial independence is a great gift to your kids. It ensures that you will not become a burden to them in your old age, and also puts you in a position to help your kids or grandkids down the line.

Make sure you are meeting your Savings Ratio, Capital to Income Ratio, and debt-reduction goals before you start allocating money to your kids' education. If you follow the ratios, there should be money available to set aside for college funds. That is one of the main reasons why the Mortgage to Income Ratio is lower than what most people currently spend on a house. The ratio has to be low enough to give you room to meet your other obligations, such as saving some money for college.

While you may not be able to save 100% of the costs of college, whatever you can save will lower the amount of debt your kids may need to take on to get educated.

## Auto Debt

"Will taking on debt to buy a car help move me from laborer to capitalist?"

Most people need a car to get to work. Thus, a car can help you make more money. You also need a car to operate your household, go to the grocery store, run the kids to soccer practice, and visit Aunt Edna once a year. But in that sense, the car is an expense. It doesn't help you make money; it helps enhance your lifestyle. This doesn't mean you should go without, it just means you must recognize a car serves a dual purpose—similar to a house. The less you spend on a car, the more cash flow you will have for savings. If you can save more, you will move from being a laborer to a capitalist that much faster.

When it comes to cars, you can spend $10,000 on a used Honda or $100,000 on a Mercedes. They will both get you to work. But if you spend a great deal on a car, you are just making the car company and their lenders richer. Money is coming out of your bank account and going to theirs every month. Now they can buy the big cars, retire early, and you will still be working. Oh, and that car you bought will be worthless after a few years.

Cars are "wasting assets." Ultimately, they are all worthless. So why spend a great deal of money on something that you know will be worthless? Would a capitalist incur debt to buy an asset that will be worthless after six or seven years? No. A good capitalist will spend just what is necessary to obtain a reliable car that will facilitate his ability to get to work and earn a living. Anything more is a luxury, and you should only spend more if you are easily meeting your 12% to 15% savings goal and are reducing your mortgage debts as required by the Money Ratios.

Unfortunately, many people are buying cars that cost $25,000 to $35,000 on household incomes of less than $100,000. This makes no financial sense. If you have two $30,000 cars, you have just spent $60,000 on cars. You could easily be spending $800 to $1,000 a month on car payments. That is 12% of your income, or equal to what you should be saving in your retirement plan. That's crazy.

However, let's say that you decide to cut your auto expenses and save another $4,000 a year in capital. Over your working career, you could easily accumulate another $400,000 to $500,000 of additional retirement assets in today's dollars, assuming the 4.5% real rate of return. This is not a hard choice. Go with the less expensive, reliable car, and dedicate the extra cash flow to building your capital. Take the emotion out of "car lust" and think about how much better it will be to have all the money you need at 65—or maybe earlier— when others are still working.

Also, don't compare your car with other people's cars. Odds are if they're tooling around in a $75,000 Cadillac Escalade, they probably can't afford it. Drive a car that will not inhibit your ability to build your personal capital. The cheaper the car, the faster you go from laborer to capitalist.

One last thing: do not get into financing or leasing a car for longer than the useful life of the car. To bring down the payments, dealers will lease or finance cars for six or seven years. Think about it. Assume you want to buy a new car that costs $25,000. If you finance it over 4 years at 7% interest, the car payment is $598 per month. If you finance the same car over 7 years, the payment falls to $377 a month. This looks cheaper. But in actuality, the first car costs a total of $28,735 and the second $31,694 because you were paying interest for three more years. Moreover, by the end of seven years, the car will be a bucket of bolts. When you go to trade it in, the dealer will ask you to pay him $20 to take it off your hands.

Plus, cars are expensive: maintenance, gas, insurance, registration, and on and on. Take my advice: go simple. Don't allow car expenses to cut into your Capital to Income, Savings, or Debt Reduction ratios. This will help you move from being a laborer to a capitalist faster.

## Credit Card Debt

The answer is "No!" The question, of course, is our usual Unifying one:

> "Will credit card debt help move me from being a laborer to being a capitalist?"

Credit card debt is the worst kind of debt and should never be incurred. Credit card companies exist to make money off you through finance charges, late fees, all kinds of arcane charges, and ridiculous rate increases. Sure, we all have credit cards and once in a while we hit a tough spot where we have to use them for something big. Fine. But pay the balance in full as soon as you can and only carry a balance on the card in an emergency. Because at interest rates that can go from 15% to 25% and beyond, who do you think is moving from being a laborer to a capitalist? It's not you. It's the credit card executives.

When you rack up credit card debt, what you are doing is pre-spending income that you do not have. Further, you are pre-spending it at a cost that is 20% higher because of the interest you will owe. While it seems like the cards allow you to spend more, they actually will result in your spending less of your future income. The repayment obligations will reduce your future paycheck and thus your ability to save money down the line. This will not help move you from laborer to capitalist.

> Example: Assume you make $60,000 a year and for the last four years you have been spending $65,000 by incurring $5,000 of credit card debts each year. At first, it seems as though the credit cards are helping you spend more and enhancing your lifestyle. But they are a silent killer, like clogged financial arteries. If you run a deficit of $5,000 a year for four years, you now owe $20,000 on your credit card. If you decide you will pay down this debt over seven years at 20% interest, it will cost you $5,330 a year, or a total of about $37,000. That's an extra $17,300 of interest that could have gone toward building your capital, but is now gone.

In summary, if debt is going to help you make or save more money in the future, then a reasonable amount of debt is acceptable.

> Mortgage debt: OK as long as it can be paid off by age 65.
> Education debt: OK, if it increases earning power and can be paid off in 10 years.
> Auto debt: A necessary evil. Keep it to a minimum.
> Credit card debt: Bad news. Avoid it altogether.

# 6

# The Investment Ratio

It's a hard time to be an investor. Markets are volatile and panic is in the air. Many people are questioning the conventional wisdom that buying and holding sound investments is the most reliable way to build long-term wealth. But is it? Or has the wisdom of 100 years been turned upside down by the events of the past few years? Let's start by asking our Unifying Question:

> "Will investing help move me from being a laborer to a capitalist?"

Probably. That's because investing is a double-edged sword. If done prudently, it can help increase your capital and move you from laborer to capitalist. But if done foolishly, it can reduce your capital and move you the other way. My Investment Ratio represents the prudent and time-tested approach to building capital over the long term. I will first cover the ratio and how it is designed to help you build and protect your capital. Then in the next chapter, I will get into a more detailed discussion about the financial markets and investing to help put the Investment Ratio in perspective.

## The Investment Ratio

There are two basic types of investments you can own: stocks and bonds. With stocks, you own a small part of a publicly owned company. With bonds, you are lending money to others with the promise that they will pay you back. Thus you can be an owner, a lender, or a little of both. One of the key questions in developing your investment strategy is, "What mix of stocks and bonds should I have?" Stocks carry greater risk and therefore offer greater potential returns; bonds are more conservative and therefore safer, but over time, your returns will typically be lower than with stocks.

The Investment Ratio sets forth the fundamental split between stocks and bonds that you should consider at different stages of your financial life cycle. This allocation will determine the vast majority of the risk you are taking and the potential return of your portfolio. It is the most important thing to get right when it comes to investing, and it is where most people make their biggest mistakes. Some investors make the error of being too aggressive and lose more of their capital than they thought possible. Meanwhile, other investors are too conservative, which reduces the likelihood that they will reach their long-term capital appreciation goals. The ratio helps you curb both of those costly tendencies.

The ratio is simple to use. Just find your age, and then the corresponding allocation to stocks and bonds. For instance, a 45-year-old should consider an allocation that is approximately 50% stocks and 50% bonds. Later we will discuss why I believe this approach, which may seem conservative to some, is actually quite prudent, even if you are young.

It is important to note that this ratio is for general education purposes and is not an individual investment recommendation. Because investment decisions must be based on your particular circumstances, I recommend that you work with a qualified financial

Here is the Investment Ratio:

| Age | Percentage of Stocks in Your Portfolio | Percentage of Bonds in Your Portfolio |
|---|---|---|
| 25 | 50% | 50% |
| 30 | 50% | 50% |
| 35 | 50% | 50% |
| 40 | 50% | 50% |
| 45 | 50% | 50% |
| 50 | 50% | 50% |
| 55 | 50% | 50% |
| 60 | 40% | 60% |
| 65 | 40% | 60% |

advisor to determine how to invest your savings. I cover how to find an advisor in the "Getting Professional Help" chapter. The Investment Ratio provides you with a framework for understanding risk and return that will help you work with an advisor and make more informed investment decisions. You may ultimately decide that you would like to follow the ratio, but this decision should only be arrived at after you have considered your individual circumstances and objectives.

## Playing Offense and Defense

The Investment Ratio is a combination of offensive and defensive strategies. The offense comes from the stocks and the defense comes from the bonds. Offense helps you build your capital and defense helps you protect the capital you have. You need both to be a successful investor. The Investment Ratio is designed to help balance the prospects for higher returns against the risk of loss.

Before we get into the numbers, it's important to define the words "stocks" and "bonds." They are thrown around a great deal, but many investors don't really know what they mean. When I reference the stock market, I am referring to the Standard & Poor's 500 stock index. This is an index that tracks the performance of 500 of the largest U.S. companies since the mid-1920s. Because it covers 500 companies, it is generally recognized as the best measure of how the stock market is doing. Although you cannot invest directly in the index, there are many investments that are structured to track the index. You'll find more detailed information on stocks and bonds in the next chapter.

When I reference the bond market, I am referring to intermediate-term U.S. Treasury bonds. These are U.S. government bonds that generally have a five-year maturity, which is the date when the bond issuer pays back your principal. We can also look at the history of these bonds going back to the mid-1920s. The reason I use U.S. Treasury bonds is because these bonds are considered the safest investment in the world. Investors assume that there is no risk of loss associated with owning U.S. Treasury bonds because the U.S. government always pays its debts. If you buy the bonds and hold them until they mature, you are guaranteed to get all of your money back in addition to the annual interest payments. Investors can purchase these bonds individually or through various investment products. There are other types of bonds that you can own, and we will talk about that later in the investment section. But for purposes of the Investment Ratio, we will assume that our bond portfolio consists of intermediate-term U.S. Treasury bonds.

What we know from the long-term history of the financial

markets is that stocks have provided a long-term return of about 9.5%, while bonds have provided a long-term return of about 5.5%. While past performance is no guarantee of future returns, these numbers provide us with the best evidence for estimating future long-term returns. These historical return numbers are an important part of the assumptions that go into the Money Ratios.

For instance, if I assumed you would get a 9.5% return on your investments, you could afford to save less because the high returns would help you build your capital faster. At an assumed 9.5% return, your Savings Ratio would drop to about 7.5%. That is a lot easier than saving 12% to 15%. The problem with this return assumption is that you would need to invest 100% of your capital in stocks. While stocks provide an opportunity for greater returns, they also carry the risk of much bigger losses. If you get hit with a big loss when you have a lot of capital at risk, you could destroy your chances of moving from laborer to capitalist.

To date, the worst decline in the stock market occurred during the period from 1929 to 1932, when the stock market declined about 80%. Since then, we have had three other declines of about 50%:

1. During the 1973–74 recession.
2. From 2000 to 2002 after the dotcom bubble burst.
3. The third started in 2007 and wasn't over as of this writing.

In between these large declines, the stock market routinely declines 10% to 20%. This is what makes stocks so risky. You can experience large declines and you cannot determine when they are going to occur. Thus, you have to be prepared to handle declines of at least 50% for whatever percentage of your capital you have invested in stocks.

So why take any risks with stocks? Why not just use U.S. Treasury bonds since there is no risk of losing money? You could adopt this approach. But because the assumed return for U.S. Treasury bonds is much lower, you will have to save a great deal more. The long-term return from U.S. Treasury bonds is about 5.5%. At a 5.5% assumed rate of return, your Savings Ratio would have to jump to about 22% to 25% of pay every single year. For many people, this is just not possible.

So if you are too conservative, you may not reach your long-term goals. If you are too aggressive, a big stock market decline could destroy the majority of your capital. A better approach is to combine the two asset classes, to use the stocks for their potential long-term returns and use the bonds for their stability and consistent interest payments. This way we can afford to take some risks with stocks because we are balancing the potential declines with the amount we have in bonds. This is the combination of offense and defense needed to manage financial risk.

## Realistic Numbers

You will recall in the discussion about the Capital to Income Ratio that I assume your investments will earn a 4.5% real rate of return over the long run. When we add back the historical long-term inflation figure of 3%, this gets us to a return of about 7.5%, which is right in between our 5.5% bond and 9.5% stock returns. This assumption is consistent with a portfolio that is about 50% stocks and 50% bonds. Pretty basic, don't you think? It's also designed to take the emotion out of investing, because most of us are primed to think only about the potential gains we will realize if stocks increase in value, but we don't want to think about the potential losses.

There is a basic relationship between risk and return in these numbers. For example, when you use only U.S. Treasury bonds, the long-term return has been 5.5%. Your risk of losses is basically zero if you hold the bonds to maturity. When you use all stocks, the long-term return has been 9.5%. That's a difference of 4% per year.

To get that extra 4%, you need to basically use an all-stock portfolio. If you do that, you open yourself up to the potential for at least a 50% decline at any time. Essentially, for every 1% return you seek above typical U.S. Treasury bond returns, you expose yourself to at least a 12% potential loss in your portfolio. So to reach for the extra 4%, your capital is exposed to risk that could, if you bet wrong, cost you half your capital if the market takes a sharp decline, as it has since 2007. That is unacceptable risk for many people.

On the other hand, for each 1% of extra return you can earn over your working years, you can lower your savings rate by about 3%. This is why the trade-off between risk and return is so difficult for people. It is nice to get a higher return because it lowers the amount you need to save. But if you reach for too much extra return, you could wipe out the majority of your capital. This is why I recommend a balanced approach. You can reach for a couple of extra percentage points of return, but not expose yourself to huge declines.

If you take another look at the Investment Ratio, you'll notice that the Ratio starts at 50% stocks and 50% bonds and stays that way through your mid 50s. It is a basic balance between offense and defense. Then, as you build more capital and get closer to the time when you want to live off your capital, the percentage in stocks declines and the percentage in bonds increases. The reason you should consider reducing your exposure to stocks as you age isn't because you are old. It is because you have a lot of capital at risk and need to live off the returns of that capital. If you lose the majority of your capital, you lose the ability to generate income. Thus, you should incorporate more defense than offense at that stage of your life.

So why have any money in stocks after you retire? Because you still have a long life expectancy. Once you're retired, the risk is not that you will die at 70. That is easy to handle from a financial standpoint. The risk is that you will live to 95 or 100 and run out of money. Life expectancy is increasing every year. With inflation, over a 30-year retirement, your distributions will likely need to at least double to give you the same standard of living at 95 that you had at 65. If you are planning on distributing 5% of your money when you first retire, by the time you are in your late 80s, you will need to withdraw an amount closer to 10% of your original account balance, due to inflation. Your capital can vanish pretty fast if you haven't increased your total pool of capital throughout your retirement years.

If you use only bonds, it is highly unlikely that you will keep up with the effects of inflation and taxes. Let's crunch the numbers:

If you start at a distribution rate of 5% and increase that for 3% inflation, after about 10 years, your distributions will have increased to about 6.7% of your retirement plan.

a. If you are earning only 5.5% on your bonds, then you will start to spend your capital. As you spend your capital, there is less available to produce income next year, but your distribution has to go up again to keep up with inflation.

b. Once this cycle starts, your capital declines relatively quickly. If you live into your 90s, you may have spent most of your capital. Thus, if you would like to attempt to keep up with inflation, you will likely need to keep some stock holdings for their potential long-term return. Once you retire, you are still a 20- to 30-year investor, at least for some of your money. This is a long enough time horizon to justify some percentage in stocks. Don't make the mistake some people make of thinking that once you retire, your active investment life is done. It's not. You still need to plan for decades in the markets.

Let's bring together the Capital to Income Ratio and the Investment Ratio. Now you can see the full spectrum of capital accumulation and risk management. The chart illustrates how much capital you should have accumulated at your age and how you should consider investing that capital.

## INVESTMENT RATIO

| Age | Capital to Income Ratio | Percentage of Stocks in Your Portfolio | Percentage of Bonds in Your Portfolio |
|-----|-----|-----|-----|
| 25 | 0.1 | 50% | 50% |
| 30 | 0.6 | 50% | 50% |
| 35 | 1.4 | 50% | 50% |
| 40 | 2.4 | 50% | 50% |
| 45 | 3.7 | 50% | 50% |
| 50 | 5.2 | 50% | 50% |
| 55 | 7.1 | 50% | 50% |
| 60 | 9.4 | 40% | 60% |
| 65 | 12.0 | 40% | 60% |

When you look at the Capital to Income Ratio, it projects a linear path on the accumulation of your capital. You start at 0.1 and slowly progress to 12 over the next 40 years. Since we never know how the financial markets will react, this is really the only way we can lay out the projected path. The reality, however, is that your Capital to Income Ratio will fluctuate each year depending on the markets. In good markets, your Capital to Income Ratio may expand quickly, and in bad markets it will decline. That is the nature of financial market returns. The Investment Ratio is designed to help reduce that volatility so you have more stability in your capital and have a better sense of the capital you are building. *Annual volatility is not as important as your long-term trend.* As long as you are constantly saving, and using a balanced investment approach, the odds are good that you will continue to grow your Capital to Income Ratio as you age and be in a position to retire by your mid 60s.

## Avoiding Large Losses

When you read stories about people who have lost their life's savings in the markets, it is generally because they have violated the fundamental strategy of balancing offense and defense. So why do people fail to implement a prudent approach to the management of their capital? One reason is because investors often want a shortcut to wealth creation. They implement a strategy that is almost all offense and fail to incorporate any defense. They see big stock market returns and are seduced by the promise of easy money. But when the markets unwind, they have little to no protection.

Another reason is that Wall Street is generally pushing investors into more aggressive strategies. It is easier to attract money when you promote strategies that look like they will provide a shortcut to greater wealth. Generally, you want to ignore what Wall Street is pushing, focus on the fundamentals, and measure yourself by your own standards. See the "Ignoring Wall Street" chapter for some basic advice on this.

At its core, investing is all about risk management. Nobel Prizes have been won and economic geniuses crowned because people developed new and better ways to assess, analyze, and capitalize on risk. Risk is the irreducible element of investing and the Investment Ratio is all about managing risk. If there were no risk, investing would be easy. All you would do is select the investment with the highest return. But it doesn't work like that. The higher the potential return on an investment, the higher the potential for you to lose your money. As you seek higher returns, you open yourself up to greater losses.

One of the most important concepts for every investor to understand is this:

Losses do more harm than gains do good.

This is why it is so important to include a healthy dose of defense in your portfolio at all times. Let me explain. If you lose 50% of your money one year and then gain 50% the next year, how much do you have at the end of the two years? You don't have all your money back. You only have 75% of your money back, even though you experienced the same percentage loss as you did gain. This is because losses do more harm than gains do good.

> Example: If you start with $100 and lose 50% your first year, you have $50 left. Now you get a 50% return on the $50, which is a $25 gain. At the end of the two years, your portfolio is worth $75, 75% of what you had when you started. The concept works the same way even if you get the gains first. Assume you start with $100 and gain 50% your first year. This means your account is worth $150. Now in the second year, you lose 50%, which takes your account value down to $75—again, 75% of what you started with.

Losses do more harm. Remember that. Smaller losses are pretty easy to handle. The real threat to your ability to go from laborer to capitalist is a large loss. By a large loss, I mean a decline in your portfolio of more than 40% to 50%. These types of declines are very difficult to recover from, especially if they happen later in your working career.

The following chart is one of the most important charts in the book. It illustrates the fundamental relationship between a loss and the future return needed to recover from that loss:

| Loss | Percentage Return Needed to Recover Loss |
|------|-------------------------------------------|
| 10% | 11% |
| 15% | 18% |
| 20% | 25% |
| 25% | 33% |
| 30% | 43% |
| 35% | 54% |
| 40% | 67% |
| 45% | 82% |
| 50% | 100% |
| 60% | 150% |
| 80% | 400% |

The left-hand column illustrates a potential loss. For instance, the first loss listed is 10%. The right-hand column illustrates the future return you need to recover the money you just lost. So if you lose 10% of your money, you need an 11% return in the future to make it back. Assume you start with $100 and lose 10%, which means you have $90. To get back to $100, you need an 11% return on the $90 ($90 × 1.11 = $100). That isn't too bad. Thus, when I mentioned that all losses or declines are not a problem, this example helps illustrate the concept. A modest decline only requires a modest future return to get back to even. For losses of 25% or less, the future return needed to get your money back isn't too much more than the loss itself. For instance, at a 25% loss, you need a 33% future return to get back to where you started.

But as you go down the chart, the numbers get scary. As the

losses get larger, you need proportionately more returns to get back to even. This is because as your capital shrinks, you have less money to build on and provide returns. Look at the 40% loss. It takes a 67% future return to get back to even. If you lose 50%, you need a 100% future return. Think about that for a minute. If you double the loss, from 25% to 50%, you triple the amount of future return needed to recover. If you go from a 50% loss to a 60% loss, your recovery percentage jumps from 100% to 150%.

This is why losses are so insidious. It gets exponentially harder to recover from each percentage decline in a portfolio. Now, all investing involves a risk of loss or decline in portfolio value. The question is how do you invest for future potential gains, without exposing yourself to a crushing decline? The answer is, it all comes down to the asset allocation you use. That fundamental split between stocks and bonds will help you manage this risk and avoid large losses. This is why the Investment Ratio is all about the allocation between stocks and bonds.

## Running the Numbers

If you have an account that is balanced between stocks and bonds, you can quickly estimate your downside exposure in your portfolio by running a few basic numbers. Remember, because we are using U.S. Treasury bonds, we don't have any risk of loss with this part of our portfolio if we buy and hold the bonds until maturity. But on the stock portion, we have to assume we could lose at least 50% at any time. I will use a $100 portfolio because it is easier to follow the numbers. At 50/50, this means you have $50 in stocks and $50 in bonds. If your stocks fall 50%, that means your stock portfolio goes from $50 to $25. If your bonds are stable, then you still have $50 in bonds. When you add the two together, you end up with $75 ($25 + $50), or a 25% decline in your account.

While this is an uncomfortable decline, it is manageable and survivable. There is a big difference between a 25% portfolio decline and a 50% decline. If you lose 25%, you need a 33% future return to get back to where you started. But if you lose 50%, you need a 100% future return to recover. At an assumed 7.5% future return, it takes about 3.75 years to recover from a 25% decline, but over nine years to recover from a 50% loss. If you're close to retirement age, that's an uncomfortable difference.

By having half of your money in U.S. Treasury bonds, you are ensuring that you cannot lose more than 50% of your capital, even if your stocks went to zero. The worst decline in the history of the stock market to date has been 80% during the Great Depression. In a 50/50 account, that means your stocks would fall to $10 and your bonds would still be worth $50, for a total of $60, which is a 40% overall decline. This is a tough result, but considering where the rest of the world would be, it is manageable and survivable.

To recover from a 40% decline, you would need a 67% future return. If you earned 7.5% on your money, it would take about seven years to recover. But if you lost 80%, you would need a 400% future return. At 7.5% a year, that would take about 22 years— assuming there are no more major market downturns, which is not a bet anyone would take. In that case, you might not recover in time to retire.

This is why defense is the most important part of your portfolio. If you don't have it, you can expose yourself to such a big decline that you can't replace your lost capital within any reasonable period of time. If you lose too much capital, then you can't transform yourself from a laborer to a capitalist. This asset balance also provides you with more control over your capital. If you have no defense in your account, and you could lose 50% at any time, then you don't really know what your Capital to Income Ratio is. If it was at 10 at the start of the year, it could be at 5 within 12 months. This is just too much uncertainty over your wealth to allow you to do any planning. Your capital could fall significantly and then it may take a decade or more to get it back.

But if you build in a healthy dose of defense, your declines are at least cut in half. Also, your recovery is even faster because you are reducing your losses. As you get closer to retirement, you see the stock allocation declines to no more than 40%. That means that if you are unlucky enough to get hit with a 50% stock decline at age 60, you will only lose 20% of the value of your total portfolio. This is a manageable decline. Your Capital to Income Ratio declines, but you still have several years of savings and potential earnings to recover. At a 7.5% future return plus your savings, you could recover in about 2.5 years. Even if the markets did not recover quickly, you could still manage through this type of volatility. The vast majority of your capital would remain intact.

You might be wondering why I have spent so much time talking about negative returns. Well, first of all, in light of the way the economy has performed in recent years, negative returns are clearly a reality. In finance, you must understand how much you can lose before you can make a decision about whether the potential gains are worth the risk.

## Forget Numbers, Know Your History

We have just gone through a difficult decade in the stock market. Lots of money has been lost on stocks and people generally feel pretty bad about their investments. It is important to remember that you don't want to assess the return potential from stocks or bonds from just one ten-year period. You need to look at the last 100 years.

Over the last 100 years, we have had peace, wars, inflation, deflation, recessions, and boom times. By analyzing financial market returns through all these cycles, you get a better sense of what you might experience as the economy and markets change over your 60 or more years as an investor. These are the long-term trend numbers that you should focus on.

It is fair to say that the stock market will likely produce much better returns in the future. And we will probably have some big bull markets ahead of us. The tough part for you will be to maintain the Investment Ratio discipline through the good times. Sometimes, markets can produce good returns for 10, 15, or 20 years, and people begin to think we have entered a new paradigm. When times are good and money is easy, people often forget about the risks in stocks. They let their stock allocation creep up to 70%, 80%, or 100% of their capital. Wealth is quite seductive and it causes people to abandon their discipline. But the risk eventually rears its ugly head again; thus you need to have your defense built into your portfolio at all times.

Every massive decline has come after a big bull market in stocks. The Great Depression came after the Roaring 20s, the 1973–74 decline came after the big bull market of the late 1960s and early 1970s, the 2000–2002 decline came after the technology boom, and the 2008 decline came after the real estate and finance boom. The risk is always there; investors just don't always recognize it.

Big bull markets also tend to come after big bear markets. The bull market of the 1920s came after a big bear market during World War I, the bull market of the mid-1940s and 1950s came after the Great Depression, the 1982 to 1999 expansion came after the terrible 1970s, and it is likely the next bull market will emerge from the wreckage of the technology, real estate, and finance collapse. The Investment Ratio will help you stay focused on the long term and help to prevent you from reacting out of either fear or greed. Balance and discipline are the two most important characteristics of a successful long-term investment strategy.

A dangerous aspect of finance that has emerged over the last 20 years is the reliance on mathematical formulas to predict market behavior. Investors who subscribe to these theories use complicated computer models to attempt to predict how humans *should* react to certain events in the markets. They believe that math can predict the actions of people just like it can predict the action of molecules. They are attempting to make finance into a hard science.

This is a fool's game. The heavy reliance on computer models is one of the main causes of the housing and banking collapse. The models failed to predict how people would actually react. This is because many economists have assumed that humans are "rational actors," meaning that, given a set of conditions, most people will react in a predictable way. But that's not the case. Humans aren't molecules. We have free will, hopes, fears, and flights of inspiration and madness. This is what makes predicting human behavior so hard. These math-obsessed investors would have been better off studying the history of the markets than designing mathematical models. Once you study the history, you see that people do crazy things. They can get wildly optimistic and wildly pessimistic, and you generally cannot predict how or when they will change their minds. You also cannot predict how greed will make some people act unethically or illegally.

If you want to be a good investor, you don't need to be great at math or accounting. What you need to know is history. Finance is not a hard science like physics or chemistry. Finance is a social science like politics. Those who have the most insight generally know a great deal about the history of the markets. You cannot prove something in finance the way you can prove it in physics. Valuations and the direction of markets are dependent on how humans interact with each other and what people believe. The value of what you own is dependent on what others think it is worth. If everybody gets enthusiastic at the same time, the value of what you own can grow quickly in the markets. But if everybody gets pessimistic at the same time, the value can fall quickly.

Understanding the history of human optimism and pessimism in the financial markets provides you with good insights into the range of things you may experience going forward. Often, the markets experience tremendous swings in valuation because investors as a group become extremely optimistic or extremely pessimistic. People have been greedy and fearful about a lot of things over the years. The objects of our obsessions change with the times: railroads, broadcasting companies, oil, the Internet, real estate, banks, gold, and even tulips.

There is a speculative nature to finance and it is what keeps the system moving. People want to grow their wealth and improve their lives. They are willing to take some risks to do this. Their willingness to invest provides capital to businesses to allow them to engage in endeavors that will, they hope, create more wealth. The system works best when people take prudent risks and then balance those risks with more conservative strategies. This allows us to try to advance without being wiped out in the process.

What often happens, however, is that people take too much risk during the good times. Then, when attitudes and markets change, they lose it all. This boom-and-bust cycle can be very destructive, as we have seen recently. If you understand the nature of these cycles, then you can elect to participate in a prudent fashion—take advantage of the booms but don't let the busts do you in.

Smart financial professionals know that you cannot predict human financial behavior with any degree of accuracy. So you don't bet the ranch on what you think other people will do in any given circumstance. Don't get me wrong; economic and financial models are very helpful in understanding the markets. They give us a rough sense of what may happen and help us organize our financial world. Where things get dangerous is when investors think the model can precisely predict the future and they make large bets on these predictions. When the model is off (which eventually it will be), they lose lots of money.

At the end of the day, simpler is better. A basic balance between offense and defense allows you to participate in the wealth-building capacity of our society without having to predict exactly how or when it will happen.

## Having a Plan B

I have mentioned that, over the long term, the stock market has returned about 9.5% per year and U.S. Treasury bonds about 5.5%. It is important to take a closer look at these return figures so that you have a better sense of what you might experience in the financial markets.

Although stocks have averaged about 9.5%, they have gotten there via the scenic route. In fact, if we look at the stock market returns over the last 100 years, rarely does the stock market have an annual return within 1% of the 9.5% long-term average.

Let me give you a simple example of what this means. Suppose you have two bricks: one that weighs 10 pounds and one that weighs 30 pounds. When you add the two together, you get 40 pounds worth of bricks. Since we have two bricks, the average brick weighs 20 pounds. But, neither brick actually weighs 20 pounds. This is the problem with averages. When there is a big difference in the size of things we are measuring, averages can be misleading.

This is similar to the stock market. There are big differences among the returns in any given year, which makes the average number somewhat misleading. While the average return is 9.5%, we don't have many years that actually return 9.5%, or even close to that. We usually get a +20%, −10%, etc., and when you average them all out, it gives us an annualized number of 9.5% over about 100 years. But that average number doesn't tell you much about what you can expect in any given year or shorter-term cycle.

For instance, the best calendar year in the stock market was a +54% and the worst was a −44%. Those numbers aren't anywhere near the 9.5% average. Moreover, the best 10-year period was a +20% and the worst was about a −1.4%.

By the way, the best 10-year period was in the 1950s; the worst 10-year period ended in 2008.

The same is true with 20-year periods. The best 20-year period was a +17% (1980 to 1999) and the worst was a +3% (1929 to 1948). Although both cycles were positive, they are well above and well below the average of 9.5%. This is about as much as you can say about risks in the stock market. It doesn't lend itself to any more precision. You just never know what you might experience, but the good years generally far outweigh the bad years over longer-term cycles. If you are prudent about how you take your risks, then investing in stocks may well be worth it to help you meet your long-term wealth accumulation goals.

What history shows us is that stock returns tend to cluster in really good cycles and really bad cycles. It is important to have the proper mind-set so that you can rationally cope with the volatility and put into place a portfolio strategy that helps you benefit from the good years but protects you in the bad. If you expect the volatility and you invest with that in mind, you are more likely to stick with your strategy over the long term and experience positive returns.

The history of financial market returns also shows us that risk changes over time. Historically, the stock market has gone up about two-thirds of the time and down about one-third. Thus, in any given year, your odds are about 66% that you will make money and 33% that you will lose money. But over a 20-year period, the odds of a loss are much smaller. There is no way to precisely gauge the probability, but in the United States, we have never had a negative 20-year cycle. That doesn't mean we won't have one, but it means the odds are relatively small, probably less than 10%. What this means is that the longer you stay with your strategy, the higher the odds are you will be successful.

Now, even though the odds are in your favor that the stock

market will go up over extended periods, we always have to recognize that there is no guarantee. While we can look at many historical cycles and get the average figures, you only get to live one cycle. Thus, we must consider the small possibility that the stock market could be stagnant for the next twenty years. In that case, we need to think about a Plan B for our capital. The Investment Ratio has a Plan B built into its structure. The Plan B comes from the income component of your returns. Let's take a look at a $100 example that's 50% stocks and 50% bonds.

> Example: We hit a 10-year cycle where the stock market
> declines by 25%. After 10 years, the $50 we had in stocks is
> only worth $37.50. But our bonds have been worth $50 the
> entire time and they pay interest each year. Let's assume we are
> getting the 5.5% return on our bonds each year. If we collect
> that interest and reinvest it in new bonds every year, at the end
> of 10 years, our bonds would have grown from $50 to about
> $85.40. When we add our $37.50 from stocks to our $85.40
> from bonds, we have a total of about $123, or 23% more than
> we started with 10 years earlier.

This is the Plan B. The Treasury bonds serve as a source of consistent income that can help you build your capital, even during extended periods of stock market decline or stagnation. If your portfolio declines because of a bear market, it helps to think out 10 years and ask yourself if you are likely to lose money over that 10-year cycle. If you have at least half in U.S. Treasury bonds, it is unlikely you will have less capital at the end of that 10-year cycle, even with the stock decline. Just let the interest on the bonds accumulate in your account and the account will likely be worth more than when you started 10 years ago.

Let's take this example to an extreme:

Assume that we have a 20-year period where the stock market declines 50%. If we started with $100, after 20 years, the $50 in stocks would only be worth $25. Our U.S. Treasury bonds, however, would continue to pay interest. Let's assume we get our 5.5% each year. By the end of 20 years, our bonds would be worth $146. Add the $146 in bonds to the $25 from stocks, and you have a total portfolio of $171, or 71% more than you started with 20 years earlier. This isn't a great return, but it is positive.

There is also a Plan C built into the Investment Ratio. While most people don't pay much attention to this, many stocks provide an income return each year in the form of dividends. Over the last 100 years, the dividend has averaged about 3%. During some cycles it is more and in some it is less, but on average it has been about 3%. Companies generally pay out a dividend as a way of returning some profits to investors each year. Dividends were paid by many major companies all throughout the Great Depression and have been consistently paid ever since. Thus, it is reasonable to assume that if you hold a well-diversified portfolio of stocks you will get a dividend return each year. If we go back to our $100 portfolio example, over the 20 years at a 3% assumed dividend payment, the cash from the stocks would add another $30 to your account, which would take you to $200, or about double what you started with.

## Thinking Long Term

It is important to understand these numbers because they should give you confidence that you have a smart, effective plan in place. If you take a rational, numbers based, long-term view, it is highly unlikely that you would lose money in a balanced and diversified portfolio over a 20-year period. The better odds are that you will do reasonably well on your stocks and just fine on your bonds. But if you don't, you have a Plan B and a Plan C if necessary. Eventually, when the markets do turn, you will have the capital available to participate, and it is likely your Capital to Income Ratio will grow quickly once the next bull market arrives.

Here's one more thing to consider: in all of the above examples, we are working with a static amount of money. You put $100 in the market and experience some return over the next 10 years. But that is not how you will experience the market. You will be putting in money every year. Because you are always allocating new capital, if you experience a bad stock market cycle, some of the money you invest will be invested at very low prices. Investing at these levels will help provide an extra boost to your capital when the markets do recover.

> Example: Assume we have a stock market that is valued at $100 a share and you buy one share for $100. Then the market falls 50% to $50. Next year, when you add your $100 you can buy two shares for $100. Let's now assume it takes 10 years for the market to recover and get back to $100. The first share you bought at $100 is now worth $100 again, so there is no gain. But the other two shares you bought at $50 each are worth $100 each. Thus, you put in $100 and you have $200. When you add them all up, you have $300. It is simply a matter of timing. Some money went in before the decline and some went in after. By allocating money every year, you can actually benefit from these declines once the market recovers.

This is a concept called dollar cost averaging, which means you are constantly buying small amounts of stocks and each purchase has a different cost depending on how the markets have performed at the time of purchase. Sometimes you buy in when things are expensive and sometimes when things are cheap. Because you cannot predict how markets will perform, a consistent strategy of adding capital through all market cycles generally works well. This is also an excellent argument for keeping some of your money invested in the market even when it is in sharp decline, as it has been since 2007.

Let's assume you were really unlucky and started investing in 1929, just before the Great Depression. As a part of your investment plan, you added $10,000 to the stock market for the next 30 years. How would you have done? Well, the first three years would have been pretty tough. But once the market bottomed, you were essentially buying the same companies you bought in 1929 but paying 80% less. When the markets recovered, the money you invested at the depths of the Great Depression would show the biggest gains over the next 25 years.

If you added $10,000 a year for 30 years, you would have invested a total of $300,000 of capital. At the end of the 30 years, how much would it have been worth? About $3,250,000, or more than 10 times what you contributed. You would have had to suffer through some scary times, but if you stayed focused and disciplined, you would have done quite well.

If you were adding $10,000 a year between 1929 and 1935, after six years, your account would have only been worth about $58,000—less than the $60,000 you put in. This of course would be frustrating, but thereafter the account would exceed your total contributions and you would have gone on to experience some pretty good gains. The dollar cost averaging effect is sort of a Plan D. It provides you with an opportunity for much higher gains on the capital that was invested during the decline. But remember, at all times you would be balanced between stocks and bonds. Part of your new capital is always going into both markets.

The reason you need to consider all of these cycles is so that you have the proper perspective for managing your capital. You will likely experience many cycles somewhat similar to what we have seen in the past, if you stay in the markets for 60 or more years.

## Make Risk Your Friend

Understanding the basic trade-off between risk and return is incredibly important to your long-term planning. For most investors, they need to take some reasonable and prudent risks with their capital in an attempt to meet their long-term goals. Moreover, our capital system functions best when people are willing to take prudent risks. If nobody wants to take any risk, then the system won't grow and many of us will be out of work. Not only can't we be capitalists, we won't be laborers, either. Thus, risk is healthy and positive, but it must be taken prudently. What that means is if the risk turns against you, you have to be positioned to survive and try again. When people or a country take too much risk and lose, they get wiped out and then it all falls apart. Don't do that.

It is also important to note that the most recent historical cycle in which you find yourself will likely have the most influence over your attitude toward risk. Between 1980 and 1999, the stock market produced phenomenal wealth and everyone wanted to participate. They didn't think stocks were risky at all. But as the price went higher and higher, people became more confident, just when the market was really getting much riskier. Now, after the last 10 years, people are very pessimistic and have become fearful of stocks. They don't think a "buy and hold" strategy works anymore.

The truth is somewhere in between, and this is the balance that is struck by the Investment Ratio. If you know you have a plan in place to address these possible scenarios, you are more likely to stick with your strategy and ultimately benefit from the wealth-building capacity of the financial markets. The Investment Ratio helps you participate prudently, and provides a backstop in the event the markets don't cooperate.

At the end of the day, it helps to put investment risk in context and compare it to other risks you face in life. Many people who are reading this book are married. The divorce rate in the United States is about 50%. And if you get divorced, you are basically going to lose 50% of your wealth to your ex-spouse. In a sense, marriage is a greater risk to your capital than the financial markets are. If you lose 50% in a divorce, the money isn't coming back. But in the markets, if you balance the risks and are patient, you generally recover and move on to greater wealth. Yet in the face of this risk, people get married all the time. Why, because the benefits that you get from a good marriage are worth the risk of a failed marriage.

This is true of many things in life. We take certain risks because we believe the potential benefits are worth the risk. If you insisted on a no-risk life, you wouldn't do much. It is reasonable to take risk, but the key is to manage the risk. In marriage, we manage the risk by working on our relationship. In investing, we manage the risk by being balanced and patient.

# 7

# Stocks and Bonds 101

Now that we have gone through the allocation and risk-management aspects of the Investment Ratio, I want to take some time to explain what constitutes the stock and bond markets, as they are the two main components of the ratio. You need to understand them so that you know how to invest your money in a broadly diversified manner. When it comes to stocks, if you don't understand what makes up the total market, you may end up being too concentrated in certain stocks that can create more risk for you. When it comes to bonds, if you don't understand the various aspects of the bond market, you may end up owning bonds that don't hold up in a crisis, which would ruin our Plan B.

When we analyze historical returns for stocks, we are analyzing the returns of a broadly diversified portfolio of stocks. We have traditionally used the stocks that make up the S&P 500 as the benchmark for historical returns. When you see that the stock market is up 20% one year or down 20%, what that means is that when you add up the total value of all stocks in the market, the value was up 20% or down 20%.

Within these numbers, if you look at specific stocks, you will see some up much more than that 20% figure and some down much more. If you hold a concentrated portfolio, you may find that the stock market provides one return, but you got a much different return because you owned only a few of the stocks in the S&P 500. Thus, your return may deviate substantially from the market if you are not adequately diversified. It is not a problem if your return is better, but you can't be sure of this. The bigger risk is that you end up investing in several stocks whose returns are much worse and you do severe damage to your capital.

In the market, we have *specific* risk and *market* risk. Specific risk is the risk that comes from owning one stock; market risk is the risk that comes from owning stocks in general. What you want to do is reduce your specific risk and take on more total market risk.

> Example: If, in 2008, you had all of your wealth in AIG, which was the biggest insurance company in the world, you would be very sorry. AIG fell more than 95% in value. But, if you had been diversified in a portfolio that tracked the S&P 500, you might have been down about 37%. Thus, specific risk may have cost you 95% of your money, but market risk only cost you 37%. By diversifying, you reduced your specific risk of one company doing severe damage. This is why people diversify. If you owned lots of stocks, in 2008, some actually went up in value, and others that declined fell much less than 37%. The "good" stocks helped offset the big declines of the "bad" stocks.

Stocks are risky enough, even if you hold a diversified portfolio. You have seen that markets can fall 30%, 40%, 50% or more during some cycles. You don't want to increase that risk by only owning a few companies or companies in one sector. For instance, in 1999, you could have owned 50 stocks and felt you were diversified. But if they were all technology stocks, your portfolio probably declined about 80%. If you held the total market, you would have been down by about 50%. In the most recent crisis, if you owned 50 different financial services firms, your portfolio might be down 80% as well, compared to the market being down about 50%.

Remember, to recover from a 50% decline you need a 100% return on the stocks. If your stocks fall 80%, you need a 400% return. Big difference. Thus, just owning a bunch of stocks doesn't mean you are diversified. The risk-management feature of the Investment Ratio requires you to diversify your stocks across the major sectors of the economy. This helps ensure that you will capture the long-term returns available from the stock market.

## What Is the Stock Market?

What constitutes the stock market? The stock market is the collection of all companies that are "publicly" traded. A publicly traded company is one in which anybody willing to pay the purchase price for the stock can become an owner of the company. The stocks in public companies are traded over certain stock exchanges, such as the New York Stock Exchange. The stock exchanges facilitate the buying and selling of the shares and help keep track of who owns what.

In the U.S. market, there are about five thousand publicly traded companies that you can buy. This is a good estimate of what constitutes the total stock market. When someone says the stock market was up today, that means (in simplified terms) that the total value of the stocks in the market was up. You may have heard of the two primary stock market indices: the Dow Jones Industrial Average (DJIA) and the Standard & Poor's 500 (S&P 500). They each measure different parts of the market, but the S&P 500 is generally considered the better measure of the market because it includes more companies.

The DJIA consists of only 30 companies. These companies are

selected by a group of editors who work for Dow Jones, which is a large financial publishing company (they publish *The Wall Street Journal*). So why do people consult it for stock market returns if it is only covering 30 companies and there are 5,000 companies out there to buy? Well, the DJIA tends to be a reasonable measure of how the market is doing because the 30 companies in the index are enormous companies and they represent a broad spectrum of the economy. They currently include GE, Wal-Mart, Microsoft, American Express, Alcoa, Caterpillar, Johnson & Johnson, and so on. These 30 companies are doing business all over the United States and internationally, so they tend to be a reasonable measure of how the markets and investors are generally doing.

The other reason people use the DJIA is because it was the first index created to measure stock returns. Charles Dow created it in the late 1800s and it is the most recognized index. Traditionally, it has had about 30 companies in it, even as markets continue to grow and expand. Every so often the editors of Dow Jones add or remove a company, but the composition of the DJIA is pretty stable.

The S&P 500 includes 500 of the largest U.S. companies. Thus, it includes the DJIA 30 stocks, plus 470 other stocks. This is why professional investors consider this index a better measure of how the market is doing. It covers more companies in more sectors of the economy. The companies in the S&P 500 are selected by a group of editors who work for Standard & Poor's, which is also a large financial publishing company. All of the return figures I use in the book come from the historical returns of the S&P 500.

Although the S&P 500 covers 500 companies, you know there are about 5,000 companies to buy. So why do people rely on the S&P 500? It's because the other 4,500 companies tend to be small, which means there is not as much money invested in them. If you add up all the money invested in the market, roughly 75%–80% of it is invested in the companies that make up the S&P 500. The other 4,500 companies only represent about 20%–25% of the money invested in the market. So, while the S&P 500 doesn't cover everything, it tends to cover the majority of the market and tends to be a good measure of how most stocks are doing. This index also has a great deal of historical data available to analyze, going back almost 100 years, which isn't true of the smaller stocks in the market.

There are other stock indexes that cover both big and small companies. One is the Russell 3000, which covers 3,000 of the largest companies—over 95% of all companies in the market. Thus, you can get a good sense of how the stock market is doing by consulting the S&P 500 or looking at the Russell 3000, which provides a little more insight because it also includes smaller companies.

It is also important to note that these indexes include companies in the 10 major sectors of the economy: finance, technology, industrials, health care, consumer staples, consumer discretionary, telecommunications, energy, utilities, and materials. During various economic cycles different sectors can provide different returns. Thus, you want your portfolio to hold stocks in all the major sectors so that your portfolio reflects the current strength in the stock market.

## It's International, Too

But wait . . . I have only been discussing the U.S. market. Companies that are headquartered in the United States are considered domestic companies and those are the ones that are included in the S&P 500 or Russell 3000. There are, however, many great companies headquartered outside of the United States, which we consider "foreign" investments. In fact, about half of all the money invested in stocks is invested in companies that are headquartered outside of the United States. This means that to really get a sense of how the "stock market" is doing, we should also consult the international indices.

There are broad-based international stock indices that measure how companies headquartered in other countries are performing. Wonder what these companies are? You may have heard of a few of them: Honda, Nestlé, Nokia, Sony, and BHP Billiton. These companies, of course, do a great deal of business in the United States, just as our companies do a great deal of business in their countries. The investment arena truly is a global market, and you will want some exposure to these other markets.

The major international stock market index is called the EAFE. It stands for the European, Australasian, and the Far Eastern index. The EAFE index includes major companies in Great Britain, Japan, France, Germany, Switzerland, Australia, Hong Kong, Singapore, and several other countries. Along with the United States, these foreign markets also offer good long-term opportunities to benefit from the expansion of wealth around the world. In today's global economy, the financial press often reports on how foreign markets are doing and the EAFE index is a good measure of foreign stock market performance.

## Profits Move the Markets

Investors are often surprised at how volatile the stock market can be. The volatility, for obvious reasons, can create a lot of fear. So it is helpful to get a basic sense of why the stock market swings so wildly in price. This helps you take a more rational view of the returns and stick with your basic plan.

When it comes to stocks, it is important to understand that the value of stocks is based on profits. The more profits, the more value; the less profits, the less value. As profits fluctuate, so do stock prices. Profits, however, are very difficult to predict from year to year. There are thousands of variables that go into determining how much profit a company may generate. You have to estimate revenue, costs of commodities, cost of supplies, employee wages, employee benefits, inflation, interest rates, and taxes, just to name a few. Some of these variables are within a company's control and some are not.

When the economy is fundamentally stable, more of the variables are easier to estimate. For instance, it might be easier to estimate revenue if the economy is growing slightly, or estimate employee wages if we have low inflation. A more stable economy generally makes investors feel confident about current profits and a company's ability to generate future profits. As profits rise for the companies in the stock market, the value of the stock market usually increases.

When the economy goes into a recession, however, it is becomes much harder to estimate company profits. Many things that affect a company's ability to generate revenue are now outside of its control. For instance, in the most recent crisis, the collapse of housing and the restriction of credit mean that it is hard to determine how much global demand there will be for goods and services in the economy.

If global demand is falling, that puts the revenue projections for most companies into question. If revenues fall, profits usually fall, which means stock prices fall. In a big recession, it is hard to estimate how much demand will fall, and thus hard to estimate how much profits will fall. Because of all the instability, investors become pessimistic. They assume big declines in global demand and revenue, and thus a big decline in profits. The declining profit assumptions are often reflected in declining stock prices.

Since the 1940s, the United States has gone through a recession about once every 6 or 7 years. These recessions are often the cause of bear markets. When we recover from the recessions, we often have bull markets.

## What Are Profits Worth?

The second factor that makes the stock market move is the price that investors are willing to pay for profits. What I mean is that it is not just the total profits that determine the value of the stock market. It is also what investors are willing to pay for those profits.

> Example: You have a company that generates $1,000,000 of revenue and has $900,000 of expenses; thus, it has $100,000 of profits in a year. If you were going to buy this entire company, how much should you pay for it? If you buy it, you estimate you will be receiving $100,000 of profits each year. What is that worth to you? You would need to pay more than $100,000. If you only paid $100,000 and then got $100,000 of profits your first year, you would earn a 100% return on your money. Clearly, the owner of the company wouldn't sell it to you for $100,000. He would be better off keeping the company and collecting $100,000 of profits each year. Determining how much to pay for company profits is a major part of valuing a company.

You might be surprised to learn that there is no agreed-upon price that investors will pay for profits. Investors' willingness to pay for profits swings wildly depending on whether people are optimistic or pessimistic about the future. If they are optimistic, they are generally willing to pay more because they assume companies will continue to grow and increase their profits in the future. If they are pessimistic, they are generally willing to pay less because they are concerned the profits may not hold up going forward. This optimism or pessimism greatly affects the value of the stock market.

For instance, in our example, if this company had a great product and you predicted that over the next 20 years the company would continue to grow its profits, you would likely pay a hefty sum to buy it and capture those future profits. Conversely, if the company is in tough circumstances with declining revenues and falling profits, you may feel that the company won't be able to produce the $100,000 every year thereafter, so you would pay less to own it. The same approach applies to the total stock market. When investors feel the economy is good and corporate profits will continue to grow, they pay more. When they feel the profits might fall and aren't confident about the future, they pay less.

Over the last 100 years, investors have paid on average about $15 for every dollar of profits (or earnings) in the stock market. This is a reference to the P/E Ratio you often hear about. P/E stands for the *Price to Earnings Ratio*. While investors have paid an average of $15, they have paid as little as $6 during bad cycles and as much as $35 during good cycles. That means if a company had $100,000 of profits, the price could swing between $600,000 and $3,500,000, just based on investor enthusiasm. That is a range of about 83% from the high to the low.

So we can see big swings in stock market value, simply because investors feel more or less confident about the future. Valuations are subject to the opinions of others and the markets are where investors express these opinions. This is what makes the stock market so volatile. Not only do you need to accurately predict the earnings of all the various companies in the market, you also have to accurately predict what other investors around the world would be willing to pay for those earnings. This is why we can see declines of 30%, 40%, and 50% in stock prices during recessions and then big gains of 30%, 40%, 50%, and more during economic expansions.

Investors often become too greedy or too fearful because they don't understand what drives market returns. During big booms, they pile into stocks but fail to understand that some of those gains are simply the result of investor enthusiasm. When the attitudes change, the markets can fall hard. Conversely, during recessions, they run from stocks because prices are falling and often lock in big losses. They fail to realize that a big part of the decline often comes from investor pessimism. Once investors feel more confident about the future, the valuations increase. Understanding these factors helps you understand the risk and maintain your basic, balanced strategy.

## Bonds . . . Government Bonds

You might be surprised to learn that the bond market is just as big as the stock market, meaning that there is just as much money invested in bonds as there is in stocks. The bond market is actually quite complex, with different types of bonds from many different types of issuers.

Unlike stocks, the value of a bond generally has nothing to do with profits. A bond is a loan between the borrower (the government or a company) and the lender (the investor). The investor loans the borrower his capital in exchange for a guaranteed interest payment. This is why bonds are often referred to as fixed income. Bonds (like loans) have a start date, an end date, and a guaranteed interest payment. Thus, the terms of the investment are fixed. For instance, you might buy a five-year U.S. Treasury note at 5% interest. This means you are loaning your money to the U.S. government for five years. During that time, you get 5% interest and at the end of the five years, you get your money back. This is why bonds tend to be a very conservative way to invest. But in exchange for the guarantees, your return is capped at a relatively modest interest payment.

In general, the bond market consists of U.S. Treasury bonds, U.S. Agency bonds, corporate bonds, and municipal bonds. These bonds offer different levels of safety and interest payments. Generally, the safer the bond is, the lower the interest payment. This makes sense because if you are going to take more risk you should be compensated with more interest. For individual investors, however, some of these fixed income securities are not a good fit. Many of these bonds are complex. Because they are complex, you are likely to make a mistake in this area. The basic mistake is that you buy a bond for its safety and predictability, only to find out that the one you bought isn't safe or predictable.

Consequently, for purposes of *Your Money Ratios*, we will stick with U.S. Treasury bonds, which are quite simple. The best thing about U.S. Treasury bonds is that they are seen as the safest investment in the world. Consequently, investors assume the bonds have no credit risk—the risk that you won't get paid your interest and principal. Because there is no assumed credit risk associated with these bonds, all you need to understand is the basic inflation risk. And the inflation risk can be reasonably handled by using intermediate-term bonds. With all other bonds, there is credit risk that needs to be analyzed.

A mistake in your credit risk analysis can cause you big problems in a part of your portfolio that is supposed to be safe and predictable. Thus, for purposes of the Investment Ratio, we're going to assume that you will take your risks with the stock market, and won't look to take a risk of loss in the bond market.

## Putting Together Your Portfolio

With so many investment options and with markets changing so quickly, how do you put together a balanced, diversified portfolio? Well, as I have mentioned, I think it is best to obtain some professional assistance with the management of your funds. The more that you understand about the markets, however, the better position you will be in to select an advisor who can assist you with building the portfolio you want. If you know you want a diversified portfolio, you won't agree to any strategy that isn't designed to track the U.S. and global stock markets. And if you know you want a balanced portfolio, you won't agree to a strategy that puts your money into 90% stocks.

Although markets are complex, all of the technology and complexity has given rise to a very simple type of investment that allows you to easily track the global stock markets. I've mentioned the S&P 500 and the Russell 3000. Well, there are investment products that are designed to track the performance of these indexes. They are commonly referred to as index funds.

An actual index isn't something you can invest in. It is a list of companies. But numerous investment firms have put together index mutual funds that are designed to hold the 500 stocks that make up the S&P 500 or the 3000 stocks that make up the Russell 3000, and thus come close to tracking the performance of the index. Thus, you can make one purchase and hold the vast majority of the publicly traded stocks in the U.S. market. You can also purchase index funds that are designed to track the international stock indexes, such as the EAFE. These funds hold hundreds of companies from different markets around the world and provide a tremendous amount of diversification in one portfolio.

> Because there are technical aspects to all investment securities, including the costs associated with buying and owning the securities, you should consider working with a qualified advisor who can assist you with making informed decisions that meet your needs. Don't simply rely on the name of a fund or an investment and assume it does what you want it to do. You need to be informed about the structure, costs, objectives, and risks of any security you consider buying.

You might be wondering how much of your stock portfolio to put in U.S. and international companies. This is a subject of much debate. In general, I would suggest you consider placing somewhere between 10% and 20% of your stock holdings in international markets. There are many great companies located all over the world, and other economies are probably poised to grow faster than that of the United States over the next 30 years. Many investors, however, don't feel very comfortable with foreign holdings because we tend to want to own what we know, and we know the United States. Plus, we live in the United States, where we earn our money and basically spend our money. Thus, most investors tend to have a "home-based bias" in their investments, which is just fine. The comfort with international stocks will most likely change over the years, depending on how well the rest of the world develops. From a diversification standpoint, however, it is prudent to consider allocating some of your stock holdings to international markets.

Index funds are designed to be passive holdings, meaning there is no manager of the fund making buy and sell decisions. The only thing the managers of the index fund really do is make sure the fund has the proper number of securities to track the index. Overall, the index portfolio is generally static, because the indexes don't change that much. Surprisingly, this tends to be a very good way to invest for the long term. All the numbers on stock market returns I previously covered are based on the index returns. Since this is the foundation of most of our research on the markets and our understanding of risk, it makes sense to create a portfolio that basically tracks the markets.

With this knowledge about what constitutes the stock market and the ability to invest to track broad-based indexes, you can ask some key questions to find out if your portfolio is diversified. First, you can find out how many stocks are in the portfolio you have. Index funds and mutual funds disclose this information, and if you have an advisor, he or she can explain the holdings. Also, you will want to know if you are diversified in the major stock market sectors. You generally don't want too much in any one sector. You want to roughly track the percentage that the sector represents of the entire market. Thus, if energy is 10% of the total market, it makes sense to have roughly 10% of the holdings in energy.

By knowing the right questions to ask, you can have confidence that you are investing in a diversified portfolio. Monitor your portfolio on a consistent basis. Markets are dynamic and things change. It's important to know if your portfolio is still tracking the broad markets and if your weightings are appropriate. For instance, at one time energy might be 10% of the market and then grow to 15%, and later fall to 10%. If you are working with a professional advisor,

they can do the monitoring for you, or you can do the research yourself if you feel you have the time and expertise to analyze the data.

## Bonds in Your Portfolio

When it comes to the bond portion of your account, the discussion is
much simpler because I assume that the bond portion consists of U.S.
Treasury bonds. As with stocks, there are index mutual funds that are
designed to hold intermediate-term Treasury bonds. These are generally passive holdings that invest in U.S. Treasury bonds and pay out the
interest to you. U.S. Treasury bonds can be bought in all types of dura-
tions from as short as 30 days to as long as 30 years, and you can buy
individual bonds if you like. The longer the term of the bond, the more
interest you can receive. But because interest rates can fluctuate significantly with inflation, it can be dangerous to own long-term bonds.

> Bond prices fluctuate based on changes in interest rates and
> inflation. Don't overreact to the movements; just understand
> how inflation can affect bond values. Assume you buy a
> $10,000 20-year U.S. Treasury bond that pays 4% interest.
> This means you will receive $400 in interest every year for 20
> years. The total interest you will be paid is $8,000 ($400 × 20
> years). Now assume that you buy your bond in the morning,
> but for some reason, on that same day, interest rates go up
> to 5%. That means an investor can buy a new 20-year U.S.
> Treasury bond and get 5% interest, instead of the 4% you are
> getting. Thus, the new bond pays $500 a year for 20 years, or
> a total of $10,000 in interest—$2,000 more than the $8,000
> you are getting on the same bond. In the market, bonds are
> priced every day to show you what you could sell the bond for.
> Because interest rates went up, your bond goes down in value.
>    Now, let's assume the next morning, you decide you want

to sell your 4% 20-year bond. An investor will not pay you $10,000 for it because he can buy a new 20-year bond for $10,000 that pays 5%. So your bond is less valuable. The longer the term of the bond, the more it will change in value if interest rates go up or down. If you have to sell a bond before it matures, you can lose money if interest rates have gone up, because your bond is less valuable. That is why you should consider buying bonds that you intend to hold until they mature. If you don't have to sell them, you can ignore the price movements. Because interest rates are volatile, it is prudent to own intermediate-term bonds. You are more likely to hold them until they mature because the time frame is shorter. If rates change, you will be getting your money back and can buy a new bond at the current rates.

If you own a 30-year bond that pays 5% and inflation jumps to 12% like it did in the early 1980s, you will be missing out on the opportunity to invest in higher-rate bonds and keep up with inflation. Thus, owning intermediate-term bonds tends to be a good strategy. The bonds mature in four to seven years, and when they mature, you get to invest the money in new bonds. If interest rates have gone up, you can buy new bonds at the higher rate. This is important because inflation is a real threat to bond returns. You need your interest payment to be a few percentage points more than inflation to get a "real" return on your money. Because interest rates and inflation can swing significantly from one economic cycle to the next, it makes sense to not lock yourself in to a long-term fixed interest rate.

It is important to remember that, just like with stocks, you should be "dollar-cost averaging" your bond purchases. This means you are buying new bonds each year as you add to your retirement savings. As interest rates change, you are capturing the different interest rate payments in each economic cycle. When rates are high, you are buying new bonds that pay a higher interest amount. And when rates are low, you are buying bonds that pay a lower interest amount. As long as you are buying some new bonds each year, you will essentially capture the interest payments available in the bond market over the long term, without trying to time the market.

The value of the bonds you own will move up and down each year as the interest rate environment changes. But as long as you hold them to maturity and you are buying some new bonds each year, the movement in price as a result of interest rate changes isn't anything to get concerned about.

There is another type of U.S. Treasury bond that is also helpful in retirement plans: a *Treasury Inflation Protected Security*. This is a unique type of bond that actually goes up in value with the consumer price index. The bonds are a little complicated to understand, but they can also fit within the intermediate-term category and can serve as a good place for a portion of your bond portfolio.

There are other types of bonds to own, such as corporate bonds. These can be a good fit for some people, but you need a deeper understanding of what you are buying because, unlike the U.S. government, there is a risk of default with corporate bonds. Some companies are not a good risk, while other companies that looked good when you bought the bonds may be in dire financial shape years later. Thus, it is important to manage your holdings for credit risk. If you are going to use corporate bonds, be sure to work with a professional who has plenty of solid experience in that market.

For tax purposes, some people may want to invest in municipal bonds. Municipal bonds are generally issued by a state or local government entity. They are usually quite safe, but not as safe as U.S. Treasury bonds. There have been municipal bonds that have defaulted, and state and local government entities can get into financial trouble if the economy in the region declines. So there are default and credit risks with municipal bonds. The reason some investors use them is for their special tax treatment. Municipal bond interest is not subject to federal income tax, and if you own a municipal bond from the state in which you live, the interest is also generally exempt from state income tax. This makes the bonds attractive if you are investing money outside of a 401(k) or other tax deferred account. But, because they are income tax–free, they generally pay less interest than U.S. Treasury bonds.

The bottom line is that if you happen to be in one of the highest income tax brackets and you are investing money outside of your retirement plan, then municipal bonds may be a good option. The municipal bonds, however, don't provide the same protection that U.S. Treasury bonds do because there is some risk of default on municipal bonds. This is another segment of the bond market where professional help is recommended.

The reason I have mentioned corporate and municipal bonds is because you may be offered these options. If you are, remember the purpose of buying bonds: to provide defense to your account. If the bonds you buy are not of the highest quality, you may find that your bonds fall in value at the same time your stocks do. Even if they are of the highest quality, they can go down in value if investors get nervous about the ability of the bond issuers to pay back the bonds. Consequently, it is generally simpler and safer for most individuals to stick primarily with U.S. Treasury bonds because of the guaranteed defense they offer.

For most people, the majority of their retirement money will be in their 401(k) plans. Thus, they must build their portfolios from the investment options offered in the plan. The good news is that most 401(k) plans offer a wide array of investment options that should allow you to build a balanced and diversified portfolio. By law, 401(k) plans must offer at least three different investment options: a stable value account, a bond account, and a diversified stock account. With the improvements in technology, most plans offer far more than just three options. Many offer index type investments or other managed accounts that are designed to broadly track the stock and bond markets. Thus, you can work with your own advisor or a representative from your 401(k) provider to put together a portfolio that meets your risk profile.

## A Rebalancing Act

The Investment Ratios identify a suggested allocation between stocks and bonds. But because your portfolio composition will change as market returns rotate, you may find that over a period of time your allocation has changed. In these periods, it is good to consider rebalancing your account.

Let's assume you start with $50 in stocks and $50 in bonds. We get a good period of stock returns and that grows to $60 while your bonds are worth $50. To keep a 50/50 account, you would want to sell $5 of stocks and put that $5 in bonds. After the rebalance, you have $55 in stocks and $55 in bonds. This makes sense because you are taking a riskier part of your portfolio that has grown and converting part of that growth into more conservative investments, to stay within the 50/50 allocation. It is a good idea to reallocate at least once a year, to stay within your portfolio parameters.

But how do you treat your account if stocks go down? Should you reallocate at that point? Traditionally, investors have thought it was a good idea to reallocate, because you were buying into the asset class that just got cheaper. This is derived from the dollar cost averaging concept we covered.

Example: We have $50 in stocks and $50 in bonds. Your stocks decline to $30. The traditional approach would be to sell $10 of bonds and buy $10 of stocks, which leaves you with $40 in stocks and $40 in bonds. Now when the stocks recover, you would, in theory, get a bigger bounce in your account because you invested more as the stocks were cheaper.

This approach violates our Plan B for the Investment Ratio. The entire theory behind the Investment Ratio is to ensure that at least half (and more as you get closer to retirement) of your portfolio is rock solid, in the event we experience cycles worse than we have seen in the past. Thus, if you take your safe bonds and sell them to invest in riskier stocks, you are essentially investing more than 50% of your capital in stocks. If the market declines for a longer period of time, according to this approach, you would continue to liquidate your bonds and keep buying stocks. You wouldn't have any bonds available to implement Plan B if necessary. You would have less principal protection for your capital and wouldn't have a source of guaranteed income to continue to build your capital if stocks don't perform as anticipated.

Because you need Plan B, I suggest you not rebalance when your stocks decline. Don't increase your risk profile during these cycles. Stick with the balance, and odds are the stocks will recover at some point and get back to 50/50. Thus, my recommendation is to consider rebalancing if stocks grow, but don't rebalance if they decline. Remember, if stocks go down, you'll still be adding new capital during these cycles because you are constantly saving. So you will be buying stocks during these declines with new money, but not with the funds you already hold in bonds.

## Summing Up

The Investment Ratio is a combination of offense and defense. The offense comes from the stocks, which should help you build your capital over the long term. Because stocks are volatile and there are no guarantees, we also need a healthy dose of defense at all times. The defense comes from the bonds. By staying balanced, you are more likely to stick with your strategy through all market cycles and reduce the extreme swings in the value of your capital. Stay rational and focus on the long-term numbers. The tips to remember:

- Markets are volatile and your wealth will often fluctuate within a range of plus or minus 20%, even with a balanced approach. Don't get too anchored to a specific value. It is healthier to look at your wealth on any given day and both add 20% and subtract 20% to get a sense of what you might be worth. Somewhere in that range is a reasonable estimate.

- Finance is a social science, and values are established by opinion, not by fact. The value of your holdings will fluctuate with what other investors think. Sometimes they are extremely optimistic and sometimes extremely pessimistic. Wealth cannot be proven, and getting comfortable with the uncertainty is part of the process. But over the long term, as the economy grows and company profits increase, the markets reflect those fundamental changes. If you stay balanced, you will reduce volatility and avoid large losses. If you avoid large losses, you are winning the major battle against volatility. Bonds provide the protection against large declines and also provide Plan B if necessary. By including bonds, you are highly unlikely to lose your capital over an extended time frame and are most likely to experience good growth.

- Maintain a fundamental balance between stocks and bonds, but as you get closer to retirement, scale the risk back so you have more defense than offense. This is necessary because now you need to live off your capital, so protecting it is more important than growing it at this stage. Thus, your account is weighted toward defense, but you still have some offense to help you keep up with inflation.

- Ensure that your allocation to stocks is broadly diversified across the entire economy. This helps ensure that no one company or sector of the economy will do significant damage to your capital. Review your holdings with a

professional to make sure you understand how your money
is allocated. Rebalance each year if the stocks go up, but
don't do so if your stocks go down.

Finally, let's bring back the *Your Money Ratios* chart with all of the
ratios we have covered so far:

| Age 65 & 80% Income Replacement | | | Mortgage Debt | Education Debt | Investment Ratio | |
|---|---|---|---|---|---|---|
| *Age* | *Capital to Income Ratio* | *Savings Ratio* | *Mortgage to Income Ratio* | *Debt to Avg. Earnings Ratio* | *Stocks* | *Bonds* |
| 25 | 0.1 | 12% | 2.0 | 0.75 | 50% | 50% |
| 30 | 0.6 | 12% | 2.0 | 0.45 | 50% | 50% |
| 35 | 1.4 | 12% | 1.9 | 0.0 | 50% | 50% |
| 40 | 2.4 | 12% | 1.8 | | 50% | 50% |
| 45 | 3.7 | 15% | 1.7 | | 50% | 50% |
| 50 | 5.2 | 15% | 1.5 | | 50% | 50% |
| 55 | 7.1 | 15% | 1.2 | | 50% | 50% |
| 60 | 9.4 | 15% | 0.7 | | 40% | 60% |
| 65 | 12.0 | 15% | 0.0 | | 40% | 60% |

Now in one place you can benchmark your Capital to Income Ratio,
Savings Ratio, Debt, and Investment allocations. These are all tied
together and designed to help move you from laborer to capitalist.
By now I hope you are beginning to understand that this is all about
striking the proper balance among these competing interests and
keeping your finances in their proper proportion.

# 8

# Ignoring Wall Street

This will be a short chapter, but an important one. If you're invested in the stock market (and most people are these days), then you've been riding along with millions of others on a wild roller coaster for the past couple of years. But there is a great deal of noise and not a lot of signal, especially if you're not a financial professional. You need to understand how Wall Street works so that you know why you should ignore most of what they say when it comes to your investment decisions.

That's especially vital as the economy continues to spiral downward and the numbers on the New York Stock Exchange continue to make many Americans panic about their investments. While Wall Street does many good things, it has the potential to lead you astray and away from the fundamentals of sound investment philosophy. This short lesson on Wall Street will help you understand why you need to stick with the Investment Ratios and ignore Wall Street.

## The Street That Isn't

You may have heard reporters on the news saying, "Let's see what's happening on Wall Street today." And then they start talking about the financial markets. So what is Wall Street? There is actually a street in New York City called Wall Street. It is on the southern tip of the Manhattan Island. Many years ago, there was a wall that ran across the island to protect the first European settlers who lived in Manhattan. Once the modern streets went in, they called this street Wall Street because it sits right where the wall used to be. Makes sense to me.

It just so happens that when brokers started trading stocks in the 1790s, they gathered at Wall Street to do so. As the business in stocks grew, brokerage firms started to open up offices on Wall Street. Today, it is where the New York Stock Exchange sits and where many major brokerage firms have offices. Thus, when people talk about what happened on Wall Street today, they are referring to the financial markets. Today, though, trading is done all over the world, and brokerage and investment firms are located in every corner of the globe. "Wall Street" has become a shorthand euphemism for the entire world of high finance.

The term "Wall Street firms" traditionally refers to firms that are in the business of trading financial instruments, like stocks and bonds. In general, Wall Street firms are all about facilitating transactions to buy and sell investments. They are brokers and get paid to "broker," or process, these transactions. Thus, the more trading and transactions they process, the more they make. That is why they are interested in you. They want to entice you to trade and engage in many transactions, because this helps them make money.

While you need access to the financial markets to build your capital, you don't really need to make many transactions to go from laborer to capitalist. So, you don't need Wall Street that much. But

Wall Street lives and breathes by the number of transactions it does. So, Wall Street will constantly market new ideas and gimmicks to get investors to change what they are doing. Change means transactions, which means commissions to them. But change to you often means more expense and little to no benefit. Wall Street makes money by getting people to change. You will make money by staying the course and sticking to the fundamentals I cover in this book. So to you, Wall Street is somewhat irrelevant.

## Beware the Gimmicks

In addition to this process of trading stocks and bonds, Wall Street firms also create all kinds of other financial instruments that investors can buy. Today, Wall Street firms are combinations of investment, insurance, and banking organizations. They offer the ability to trade stocks and bonds, buy mutual funds, get life and disability insurance, get a mortgage, and open a bank account. It's like being in a financial Wal-Mart. By offering all of these products, these companies hope to get access to every dollar you spend on financial services and to keep you from going anywhere else.

But many of these financial services products are just commodities, meaning there isn't much difference among them. It's like buying corn. You can get it from Safeway or Kroger, but you're just buying corn. Because many of the products are commodities, companies need to use slick marketing to create the perception of a meaningful difference. This is where it starts to get confusing, and confusion causes investors to pursue things they do not need. The companies only make money if you make a switch from one investment to something else. Thus, their efforts are all focused on getting you to move your money from Company A to Company B.

Now, let's be clear. There will be times in your life when you need to modify what you are doing. The world is a dynamic place and all of us need to adjust. But these changes should always be based on solid reasoning and sound financial data, not marketing hype. Most marketing is targeted to your animal instincts of either fear or greed. These are the most powerful motivators in the markets. Thus, beware of marketing that appeals to those instincts.

The truth is that you should be skeptical of all financial services marketing, just like all other areas of life. That doesn't mean you don't need some of the products and services that are out there. It just means that much of what you need is fundamental, and when things start to look too complicated, your "being screwed" radar should light up like a Christmas tree.

Many times, people jump into niche or "hot" investment offerings, a funky annuity, or an elaborate insurance arrangement at the prompting of some broker, all before they ever understand the fundamentals of what they're getting into. Mortgage-backed securities, products comprising bundled high-risk mortgages, are one example. They were red-hot back in 2005 and 2006, when real estate was flying high on its ridiculous bubble. But when the market came crashing down, mortgages became worthless and so did the fancy new securities. Investors lost billions.

These fringe deals look interesting, and it is easy for Wall Street to pull in money by emphasizing some minor aspect of the deal, as if it is a major discovery. Usually, they do this around tax issues, some good but selective history of investment returns, or some guarantee that you won't lose money. If the client decides to participate, the client generally gets something that turns out not to be that special, probably costs more than they thought, and doesn't do everything that was promised. All the while, he or she is distracted from executing on the fundamentals of smart investing.

Until you master the fundamentals, you don't need to be concerned with much of what Wall Street has to say or market. Getting distracted by Wall Street's marketing will likely blow you off course, cost you lots of money, and not move you any further down the path from laborer to capitalist. Ignore most of what Wall Street says, focus on the fundamentals, and you will likely be better off in the long run. The investment strategy I discuss in this chapter provides you with the investing fundamentals that you will need to create a successful portfolio. Stick to this basic strategy and you should be fine.

## The Art of Doing Nothing

In addition to ignoring Wall Street, you will be a more successful investor if you master the fine art of doing nothing. Doing nothing is often an excellent strategy for preserving wealth, and dovetails nicely with the principle of ignoring Wall Street. In the investing world, wealth preservation is 80% of the game. Most financial wounds are self-inflicted. People get hurt in finance because they make big mistakes by deviating from the fundamentals. They lose large sums of money in short periods of time, and before they know it their financial life has been turned upside down.

Often, doing nothing is critical to financial success. Each and every day you will be tempted with some new investment, some hot topic, something to get you to move your money from Company A to Company B. Why? Because the guys at Company B will make money if you switch. We just went over this.

There is never a reason to rush into any financial decision. No matter how good you think the deal is, there is always another deal later on. Plus, if you are rushing into it because someone has convinced you it is too good to pass up (greed) or that if you fail to act now you won't get another chance at something this good (fear), you probably don't know what you are doing. So, do nothing.

The truth is that you don't need to jump from one investment to the next to be successful. Lots of moving around and changing positions is unlikely to be of much help to you. It is also expensive to move around, because you generally get hit with transaction costs and taxes which just reduce your capital even more. You should make some strategic investment changes over time, but staying the course and keeping yourself on track is the most important aspect.

Some of the smartest investors in the world have mastered the art of doing nothing. Warren Buffett is widely recognized as the best investor of all time. He is the CEO of a company called Berkshire Hathaway, which you may know about. He is great at doing nothing, and only doing something when he understands what he is doing. He will go years without making many significant changes, because he believes he has made fundamentally good choices. When you believe you have made fundamentally good choices, you have the confidence to stick with your decisions.

You may often feel as if you are losing out if you do nothing. Everyone else seems to be doing a lot of something and bragging about it. Well, don't believe everything you hear. People don't tell you about all the stupid decisions they have made, and often the ones they are bragging about turn sour later. Doing nothing is actually an affirmative choice to maintain your positions and commitment to your path. The fundamentals of investing don't change much over time, and you won't need to, either.

At its core, investing is about managing risk and uncertainty. As I mentioned, investing has the capacity to add or subtract from your capital. If you make consistently prudent decisions, odds are that your investment activities will significantly add to your capital. If you take too much risk and make irrational decisions, odds are that investing will subtract from your capital.

The more rational you are with your investment decisions, the better you will be at managing risks. You will basically increase the odds of good returns and decrease the odds of bad returns. If you block out all the noise from Wall Street and keep your fear and greed in check, the path is relatively easy.

## The Financial Press

Although Wall Street has done its fair share of contributing to financial problems, you need to be somewhat skeptical of the financial press in both good times and bad. Here's why: Because of our twenty-four-hour, seven-day-a-week news cycle, the media are always looking for a story. Finance is appealing to editors and producers because markets and the economy are always changing—they are inherently dramatic. Moreover, people need to know what is happening in the business world and financial markets. These developments affect their lives. That's all fine, and financial reporting is a good business.

There are times, however, when some in the financial press stray from their mission of reporting and informing. Where the media have problems is when they start writing about "ways to beat" the markets and make more money than your neighbors make. When they do that, they are getting into areas they often know little about and can be highly influenced by the Wall Street marketing machine. Thus, Wall Street and the financial media sometimes feed off each other. Wall Street comes up with all these great ideas that it markets to the media, and some media outlets report on them so enthusiastically that they give the appearance of *supporting* ideas as opposed to *reporting* on them.

Many financial services firms spend millions every year pitching their ideas and stories to the financial press. Some in the press grab these stories because they are prepackaged and make for good headlines that catch readers' attention. The press at times does the same thing that Wall Street does; it focuses on the most recent best-performing investments or highlights some obscure financial vehicle that will do little to help the average reader build their financial security. "Buy and Hold" and "Balanced Investing" do not make for eye-catching headlines.

## Complicated Realities

Finance is a terribly complicated business. It takes a great deal of work and research to understand what not to do. The crisis that emerged in 2008 at the big banks and brokerage firms due to securitized, subprime mortgages is a good example. I am not able to get into all of the details about securitized lending, but some aspects of these securities have actually helped lots of people. But like many good financial innovations, Wall Street took it way too far because they were hungry for bigger profits. They took a good concept and made it so incredibly complicated that few people in finance truly understand how the instruments work.

For years, the numbers looked good on these investments because of the real estate bubble, so Wall Street produced tons of them and had an army of salespeople selling them to sophisticated institutions and investors around the globe. Because they had worked in the past, everyone assumed they would continue to work. Nobody really investigated what was going on. And firms that were making big money on these deals were trotted around as investment geniuses. Well, the results speak for themselves.

As I mentioned previously, you need Wall Street and the capital markets to help you build financial independence. Much of what modern finance has created has improved the lives of billions of people around the world. And we need good financial reporting to tell us what is going on in the world and to help keep the markets honest.

The good media outlets and reporters need your support to stay in business. So if you value good, honest, and balanced reporting, express it through what you read and buy. The press should stand on the side of the reader, not Wall Street. That is when the system works best.

# 9

# The Disability Insurance Ratio

For most people, insurance is an unwanted expense and appears to have little relevance to financial success. The problem with insurance is not the insurance itself, but how the insurance is marketed and distributed. Before I elaborate, let's ask the Unifying Question:

"Will insurance help move me from being a laborer to being a capitalist?"

At first glance, it seems as though insurance premiums simply reduce the amount of money you have and thus the amount you have to invest. So, doesn't insurance serve as an impediment to wealth building? No. If used properly, insurance actually frees up more capital for you to invest and it protects the capital you have from being wiped out to pay for a large liability. For a relatively small fee, you can insure against large potential losses that would put enormous financial strains on you and your family. Thus, the proper use of insurance is necessary to help move you from laborer to capitalist.

## Basics of Insurance

Insurance companies insure against things that are unlikely to happen, but if they did happen, would create a large liability that you would have to pay. Because the event is unlikely to happen, the insurance company charges you a relatively small fee each year (the premium) compared to the potential loss you could incur. In exchange for the premium, the insurance company agrees to step in and cover your large losses should the unexpected event occur. If the event never happens, then the insurance company keeps the premium and makes a profit. If the event happens, the insurance company pays you for your loss.

If you did not have insurance, how would you prepare yourself for large health-care bills in the event of a serious illness or accident to you or a family member? You would need to save a couple hundred thousand dollars to cover a potential health-care crisis, or you would have to pray that nothing bad happened. But such things do happen. A gentleman I know had his otherwise perfectly healthy wife fall ill from an asthma attack that almost killed her. She recovered, but if they had not had health insurance, the bill would have been $150,000 or more. Because they had coverage, their total cost was $5,000.

The cash you would need to save to cover the "might happen" disasters could not be invested, because it would need to be available on a moment's notice to pay unexpected and large bills. Plus, if you do get sick, and it costs $200,000 to treat you, it could wipe out all or a sizable percentage of your personal capital. After paying the bills, you then have to replenish what you spent because you, or another family member, could get sick again in the future. Having no health insurance would require you to dedicate a great deal of your savings to a reserve fund for your potential costs, and a very large bill could wipe out everything you have.

This is why insurance was created. Now you can buy coverage in the event you have a health crisis, a car accident, or your home catches on fire. You are then free to take your other funds and invest them for the long term, knowing that you won't have to liquidate them to cover a potential, but unlikely, emergency. This is how insurance helps move you from laborer to capitalist.

The key to using insurance is to only use as much as you need to insure the risks you cannot afford to pay for yourself. At some point, when you build enough capital, you won't need certain types of insurance. Why? Because if a disaster strikes or a bad thing happens, you'll have enough money to simply pay the bills. But, between now and the point when you have a lot of capital, you need insurance to free you up to invest and to protect your savings from being wiped out along the way.

> Example: Bill Gates, the founder of Microsoft, is worth $40 billion. Does he need health insurance? No. Regardless of how sick he gets, he would never spend more than a few million dollars on his own care. This is such a small amount compared to his total wealth that he can afford to self-insure. If he stays healthy (and the odds are he will), then he has saved all that money that he otherwise would have spent on health insurance. If he gets really sick, which is unlikely, he just pays the bills. But when Bill Gates was younger and had less capital, he would have needed health insurance. If he had gotten seriously ill or in an accident at age 22, the cost of that incident may have wiped him out financially and prevented him from starting Microsoft.

But Bill Gates might need other kinds of insurance. Let's look at auto insurance. Assume Bill drives a world-class Mercedes valued at $200,000. Does he need collision insurance on this car? No. The odds of him having an accident are low, and if he has a fender bender, he can afford to pay the $25,000 to fix it. But he needs liability insurance. Let's say Bill runs down a Silicon Valley venture capitalist whose own net worth is about $4 billion. The man is disabled and can no longer work. His family then sues Bill for the lost future income. Since the man earned a huge amount of money, the exposure is very big. A court judgment could be huge. Thus, Mr. Gates might want to buy liability insurance, because it is harder to assess the potential exposure from a personal injury claim.

The moral: most people need some kind of insurance. Don't make the mistake of thinking that just because you have money you can drop all of your insurance. Some of it can be dropped as you build more capital, but some of it you may need for your entire life. The key is to drop what you don't need and keep what you do.

In this chapter, we're going to look at disability insurance. In the two following chapters, I'll discuss the other two types of insurance that are critical to moving from laborer to capitalist: life insurance and long-term care insurance.

## Disability Insurance

The most important insurance for you to have is long-term disability insurance, and I'll bet you don't have it or don't have much of it. Why is long-term disability insurance so important? Let's ask our Unifying Question:

> "Will disability insurance help move me from being a laborer
> to being a capitalist?"

To move from laborer to capitalist you need a job that produces income. You then need to save a portion of that income each year. If you are disabled and cannot work, you have no job and thus no income. Therefore, if you become disabled, it will be nearly impossible to move from laborer to capitalist. Consequently, it makes sense to insure your income stream, and that is what disability insurance does.

If you do become disabled, the disability insurance provides you with a monthly cash payment to replace your wages. These funds provide you with the income to pay for your basic living expenses, health care, and savings. Most people do not realize that they are more likely to become disabled than to die young. According to the insurance industry's own numbers, your odds of dying in a particular year are one in 106, while your odds in a given year of being disabled and unable to work are one in eight. Disability creates a huge strain on your family finances and is a very serious situation that needs to be addressed through the use of insurance.

Disability benefits are quoted in terms of a monthly benefit. For instance, you may get a disability policy for $5,000 per month. Benefits are generally payable through age 65, as long as you remain disabled. Once you reach 65, the payments generally stop. This makes sense because the payments are intended to reproduce your wages through your anticipated working career, which would generally end in your mid 60s.

If you become disabled, you will need to allocate a portion of your disability benefits to savings, because you need to continue to build capital through age 65. Remember, you will need the earnings from that capital to live on once the disability payments stop at 65. Again, that is why disability insurance is so important. Not only do you need income to support yourself in your younger years, but you also need some source of funds to build capital.

The maximum disability benefit is generally limited to about 60% of your monthly pay. There are two reasons for this. The first is that the insurance industry does not want to give you too much of an incentive to stay at home. By limiting benefits to 60% of pay, you have a reasonable incentive to figure out how to reenter the workforce. The second reason is that if you buy an individual disability policy, the benefits you receive are tax-free. Because they are tax-free, the 60% benefit comes pretty close to reproducing the after-tax income you had while working.

> Example: Assume you make $100,000 a year, which is $8,333 per month. Assume you pay income taxes of 25% on your wages, which means your net monthly pay is $6,250 ($8,333 × 75%). If you have a disability policy for 60% of your monthly income, the tax-free disability benefit is $5,000 a month (60% of $8,333). The $5,000 monthly benefit is 80% of your $6,250 after-tax pay while working. Thus, the 60% tax-free benefit comes pretty close to reproducing the after-tax income you had while working.

The following chart illustrates this:

| Gross Monthly Pay | $8,333 | Disability Monthly Benefit | $5,000 |
|---|---|---|---|
| Taxes at 25% | $2,083 | Taxes | $0 |
| Net Pay | $6,250 | Net Pay | $5,000 |

So how much disability insurance do you need? Consider getting the maximum coverage available, 60% of your income. If you become disabled, you will need money for monthly living expenses, increased health-care costs, and savings. Thus, you will likely be using all of the dollars available from that policy. Remember, you still need to continue saving because the disability payments stop at age 65. Even though you can't work, you must continue to build capital. Thus, we have the Disability to Income Ratio:

| Age | Disability to Income Ratio |
|------|------|
| 25–55 | .60 |
| 60 | .40 |
| 65 | 0.0 |

To determine how much disability insurance you should consider, take your income and multiple it by the ratio. If you make $100,000 a year, you multiply $100,000 by .60, which gives you $60,000 of disability coverage. Because disability insurance is priced in a monthly benefit, just divide the $60,000 by 12, which gives you $5,000 per month. You will need to maintain the disability coverage most of the way through your working years. But, as your Capital to Income Ratio grows, later in life you can consider reducing your coverage. You see that the ratio drops to .40 at age 60. If you become disabled at that age, you should have accumulated assets that can produce income for you. Thus, you don't need as much insurance.

> Example: Assume you make $100,000 a year and have gotten your Capital to Income Ratio to 9 by age 60. This means you have $900,000 of savings. If you become disabled, you could use the 5% distribution from your savings to cover your living expenses. This would produce about $45,000 of income a year. Because you have a good portion of your expenses covered by the earnings on your capital, you can reduce the disability coverage to 40% of income. Then, if you became disabled, you would have $40,000 from your investments and $45,000 in disability benefits. This would be enough to provide a source of funds for continued savings and get you through to age 65. I don't recommend cutting back on your disability coverage until your Capital to Income Ratio gets to 8 or 9.

Once you reach a Capital to Income Ratio of 12, you shouldn't need any disability, because the earnings from your investments are enough to sustain your lifestyle. At such a ratio, and a 5% distribution, your income is 60% of your preretirement income. This is the same percentage as your disability coverage. At this point, you can simply live off the earnings from your capital. Remember, you will also have a Social Security benefit kicking in, which should add another 20% to your retirement income.

Now, here's the ratios chart with the Disability to Income Ratio included:

| Age 65 & 80% Income Replacement | | | Mortgage Debt | Education Debt | Investments | | Disability Ratio |
|---|---|---|---|---|---|---|---|
| Age | Capital to Income Ratio | Savings Ratio | Mortgage to Income Ratio | Debt to Avg. Earnings Ratio | Stocks | Bonds | % of Monthly Income Replacement |
| 25 | 0.1 | 12% | 2.0 | 0.75 | 50% | 50% | .60 |
| 30 | 0.6 | 12% | 2.0 | 0.45 | 50% | 50% | .60 |
| 35 | 14 | 12% | 1.9 | 0.0 | 50% | 50% | .60 |
| 40 | 2.4 | 12% | 1.8 | | 50% | 50% | .60 |
| 45 | 3.7 | 12% | 1.7 | | 50% | 50% | .60 |
| 50 | 5.2 | 15% | 1.5 | | 50% | 50% | .60 |
| 55 | 7.1 | 15% | 1.2 | | 50% | 50% | .60 |
| 60 | 9.4 | 15% | 0.7 | | 40% | 60% | .40 |
| 65 | 12.0 | 15% | 0.0 | | 40% | 60% | 0% |

## Buying Disability Insurance

So how do you go about getting disability insurance? You will need to contact an insurance agent to help you get a quote for disability coverage. It can be tricky, so using a good and reputable agent is important. Generally, the agent will be able to provide quotes from several different companies. You then need to go through underwriting, which means the insurance company evaluates your health status. Disability coverage can be hard to get, so it is best to try to secure a policy when you are young and healthy.

Many policies have a feature that allows you to increase coverage later in life if your wages increase. Also, because retirement funding is becoming such a big issue, some companies are offering additional insurance coverage to make up for any lost 401(k) contributions as a result of being out of work. Generally, the companies deposit a sum of money into a trust for you that would be paid out once you are no longer disabled or reach age 65, whichever comes first. This is an interesting feature and would come in handy if you experience a long-term disability.

Policies are also providing riders for "catastrophic disability." This is an extra source of funds that would be paid to you if you become severely disabled. It is paid above the standard benefit amount and is there to help cover the additional medical costs and expense your family would incur if you become severely disabled. The retirement savings and catastrophic features can push your Disability Coverage Ratio above the 60% minimum target, which may be very valuable. Your insurance agent can help you structure the policy to meet your individual needs.

The other unique aspect about an individual policy is that it is generally tied to your ability to work in your profession. This means that you are considered disabled if you can't do a job comparable to your current job. This is a very important feature since many people spend lots of money getting educated and trained in a particular field. You want to protect your income stream for the type of work you are trained to do. If a surgeon loses the use of her right hand in an accident, she can no longer practice as a surgeon. If she has a disability policy tied to her specific occupation, she would be considered disabled. But if the policy only pays her a benefit if she is unable to work in any sort of profession (not just unable to work as a physician), she would not qualify for benefits. Why? Because she could be an accountant or a banker.

Individual policies can be expensive, but it is important to secure the coverage. There are, however, other sources of coverage that are available for disability insurance. These can be useful if you cannot qualify for an individual policy or cannot afford an individual policy for the full 60% income replacement target. The other source of disability insurance that is most common is from your employer through a group disability plan. Many employers offer their employees the ability to get long-term disability coverage under a company plan. These plans are generally much less expensive than an individual policy, and they can provide some basic coverage. But, they often have several significant drawbacks.

First, they generally have a lower coverage limit, such as offering 60% of pay up to $3,000. This means that no matter how much you make, the benefit will not be more than $3,000 a month. Often, you can't get to a full 60% of pay coverage with a group plan if you have a higher salary. Plus, the benefits are subject to income tax, as opposed to an individual policy, which is tax-free. The difference is because the employer is paying all or a part of the premium, which is an employee benefit and not taxed to you as income. Thus, if you do need benefits, the IRS taxes the payments. The tax reduces your net disability pay even more.

Plus, many group plans only cover you if you are unable to work in any occupation, and often only provide benefits for several years, as opposed to through age 65. Therefore, if you sign up for a group policy, you may think you are covered, but find out you are only partially covered. To top it off, most group plans have an offset for any disability benefits you may receive under the Social Security Disability Insurance program (SSDI).

SSDI is a federal disability program that is part of the Social Security system. Most people who have been working and paying into Social Security will qualify for an SSDI benefit if they become severely disabled, meaning they cannot engage in any gainful activity. In that case, you may qualify for an SSDI benefit. But if you have a group plan, the monthly benefit may be reduced by any SSDI payment. If you have an individual policy, however, your payments are generally not offset by an SSDI payment.

While a group plan can offer some basic coverage, there are many holes in the policies. But, they are generally cheap and don't require you to take a physical exam. If your employer offers a plan and it covers long-term disability, it is worth considering signing up if the cost is minimal. That way, if you do become disabled, you have another source of potential funding. Or, if you cannot afford to buy an individual policy to get you all the way to the 60% income replacement, then consider signing up for the group benefit to provide some additional coverage. With a group plan, however, once you leave the employer, the insurance coverage stops. Group plans can provide some basic coverage, but don't rely on them as the foundation for insuring your income stream and ability to continue to build capital.

Get yourself a good individual policy that insures you for your ability to work in your profession. Consider adding a rider to cover any lost 401(k) contributions and a rider for catastrophic benefits. These will provide some additional cash flow if you find yourself severely disabled. Then, review your disability coverage every few years, to make sure it is keeping up with any increases in your pay.

# The Life Insurance Ratio

Life insurance does just what it says: it provides a payment in the event of your death. Life insurance is very popular, but we come back to the Unifying Question:

"Will life insurance help move me from being a laborer to a capitalist?"

No, it won't. In a strictly economic sense, there is no reason for an individual to buy life insurance. Life insurance proceeds are never paid to you. They only arrive after your death, which won't do you much good. So why do we buy life insurance? We buy it for our spouses and kids. We have people who are dependent on our income for their support. If we are gone, then they will need the life insurance payment to replace our income. Therefore, it is our loved ones who need life insurance to help move them from being laborers to capitalists. Assuming you care about your loved ones being financially independent, you will need some life insurance.

How much life insurance do you need? The policy should be large enough such that the income your family could generate from the cash they receive will replace the majority of your income. You are no longer around, so the family expenses will be somewhat lower. This means the family can get by with less than what you were bringing home in salary. The amount of life insurance you need is basically the inverse of your Capital to Income Ratio. In general, you should have insurance that is equal to 12 times your pay minus your Capital to Income Ratio at that age. The Life Insurance Ratio:

| Age | Life Insurance to Income Ratio |
|-----|--------------------------------|
| 25  | 12                             |
| 30  | 11.4                           |
| 35  | 10.6                           |
| 40  | 9.6                            |
| 45  | 8.3                            |
| 50  | 6.8                            |
| 55  | 4.9                            |
| 60  | 2.6                            |
| 65  | 0                              |

To determine how much life insurance you should have at a particular age, take the ratio and multiply it by your income. For instance, assume you make $100,000 a year and are 40 years old. Your ratio is 9.6, and thus you should have 9.6 × $100,000, or $960,000 in life insurance. Let's work this out. At age 40, your Capital to Income Ratio should be 2.4, which in this example would be $240,000 of capital. Consequently, if you were to pass away at age 40, your family would have $240,000 of capital plus $960,000 of life insurance, for a total of $1,200,000, or 12 times your pay. Life insurance proceeds are not subject to income tax. Thus, your heirs will receive the entire $960,000 and owe nothing to Uncle Sam.

As you know from our prior discussions, this would produce about $60,000 worth of income for your family if they assumed a 5% distribution. This should be sufficient for two reasons. First, you are not around anymore, and from a financial standpoint this lightens the amount of income the family needs for support. Second, if you have small kids, then they may also qualify for a Social Security Survivors benefit. If you have kids in the house under 19, the kids can collect a Social Security Survivors benefit through age 19. If your spouse is caring for the minor kids, then he or she can also receive a Survivors benefit. While it will depend on the number of children you have, you could expect about a 20% Social Security benefit for your wages, up to the current $106,800 Social Security wage base. When you add up the distributions from your investments plus the Social Security Survivors benefit, your family should be close to producing 80% of your prior income, with one less member of the family to support. From a financial perspective, this should be sufficient for their financial security.

## Life Insurance Needs

Because the amount of life insurance you need is tied to your current Capital to Income Ratio, your life insurance needs decline as you get older and build more capital. Every time your Capital to Income Ratio grows by 1x pay, you can look to reduce your life insurance coverage by the same amount. When you eventually get to the Capital to Income Ratio of 12, you would no longer have a need for life insurance—at least from a retirement standpoint.

The following chart pulls together the Capital to Income Ratio and the Life Insurance Ratio:

| Age | Capital to Income Ratio | Life Insurance to Income Ratio |
|-----|------------------------|-------------------------------|
| 25  | 0.1                    | 12                            |
| 30  | 0.6                    | 11.4                          |
| 35  | 1.4                    | 10.6                          |
| 40  | 2.4                    | 9.6                           |
| 45  | 3.7                    | 8.3                           |
| 50  | 5.2                    | 6.8                           |
| 55  | 7.1                    | 4.9                           |
| 60  | 9.4                    | 2.6                           |
| 65  | 12.0                   | 0                             |

The Life Insurance Ratio assumes you are hitting your Capital to Income Ratio at each age. If you find yourself behind in building your Capital to Income Ratio, make sure you continue to maintain sufficient life insurance so that the insurance proceeds, plus what you have saved, would put your family at a Capital to Income Ratio of 12 were you to pass prematurely. If you can do that, then you will have left your family with sufficient assets to maintain their financial independence.

Example: Assume you are age 50, make $100,000, and have $300,000 saved. Thus you have a Capital to Income Ratio of 3. Ideally, you would like to have a Capital to Income Ratio of 5.2 by that age, so you are a bit behind. If that is the case, you should consider maintaining life insurance equal to 12 times your pay minus your Capital to Income Ratio of 3; in other words, you would want $900,000 in insurance. If you pass away, your family receives the $900,000 of insurance plus

the $300,000 in savings, which puts them at $1,200,000, or a
Capital to Income Ratio of 12 times your pay.

While these are general rules, each family has unique needs. For
instance, assume you are married, have no kids, and both spouses
make $100,000 a year. If you die, your spouse is still earning enough
to support him- or herself. Thus, you may not need life insurance.
Or, you might decide to each get a policy for $500,000 to help
the survivor during the grieving process. A death will always set the
surviving spouse back, and a reasonable amount of life insurance proceeds will probably be very helpful. But, you would not need the same
amount as an individual with three kids and a stay-at-home spouse.

The point is to carry a meaningful amount of life insurance when
you are young, have kids, and your savings are low. The good news is
that life insurance is pretty cheap for young people. As your assets grow
and kids leave the house, you can consider reducing the coverage.

## Buying Life Insurance

You have a good idea of how much life insurance you need. Now the
tough part: buying life insurance. I don't know many people who are
interested in talking to their life insurance agent. Again, it is not the
insurance that is the problem, it is how it is marketed and sold. Insurance salespeople want and need to sell insurance. Thus, they often
see insurance as the answer to everything. Don't like paying taxes?
Maybe you should buy some insurance. Can't find a date on Saturday
night? Maybe you would be more attractive with a large insurance
policy. If all you have is a hammer, everything looks like a nail.

Life insurance comes in two basic varieties: term and permanent. Term insurance is designed to be in place for a specific number
of years. Permanent insurance is designed to stay in place for your
entire life. Insurance agents make bigger commissions (much, much

bigger) by selling permanent insurance. Thus, when shopping for insurance, you will often be offered some form of permanent insurance. But the majority of the time, term will meet your needs.

## Term Insurance

A term policy is a policy that you take out for a term of years. For instance, you can buy a $1,000,000 20-year term policy. What this means is that if you die any time during the next 20 years, your beneficiaries will receive $1,000,000. If you die in the 21st year, they get nothing because the policy was no longer in force. Term policies can be bought for as short as one year or up to as long as 30 years, so they will cover the life insurance needs of most individuals.

When you are young, insurance is cheap because your risk of death is low. As you get older, the premiums increase. The longer the term policy, the higher the premium will be for any given amount of insurance. A 20-year policy is more expensive than a 10-year policy because you have 10 more years of coverage and you are getting older each year. Insurance premiums start to climb at about age 40 and they really accelerate after age 65. But, if you have been following the Money Ratios, you should have enough assets saved by age 65 that you won't need any insurance and can drop it just as it starts to get really expensive. In the Money Ratios, you only need life insurance until your Capital to Income Ratio reaches 12. This is why term insurance works so well for helping you protect your family's finances while you are still building your capital.

Another thing to consider is that many term policies carry a provision that allows you to convert them, or a portion of the coverage, to permanent insurance in the future, without having to go through another medical exam. This can come in handy if for some reason you become uninsurable later in life because of a health risk. Once you convert the policy, it is yours to keep for as long as you keep paying the premium. What if you buy a 20-year term policy at age 30 and get cancer at age 40? That 20-year term policy will terminate at age 50, and you may not be able to get new life insurance. If your term policy carries a conversion feature, you can convert it to a permanent policy so that you can keep the policy in place. Now, some term policies require you to convert the entire amount to permanent insurance, while others allow you to convert a portion of the term insurance. Look for policies that allow you to convert a portion, because you may not need all of the insurance and converting the entire amount may be too expensive.

## Permanent Insurance

A permanent policy is one that is designed to stay in place for your entire life. You may have heard of "whole life" insurance—this is a form of permanent insurance. The other form of permanent insurance is called Universal Life. There are some technical funding differences for these types of policies, but the essence of each type is that it is designed to stay in place for your entire life, not just a term of years. Thus, if you pay the required premiums, you will always have insurance.

In theory this sounds like a good idea, but the problem is that permanent policies are very expensive. Because they are so expensive, you may not be able to afford adequate coverage when you are younger and need the higher insurance benefits. Also, why pay for the more costly benefit if you may not need insurance for your entire life?

Permanent insurance policies are designed to have you put in more money in the early years so that you can build what is called "cash value" in the policies. Thus, you are paying a premium that is far more than the actual cost of insurance each year when you are younger. The additional money you are putting into the policy goes into an account for you. That money then generally grows over time, based on various factors, such as interest rates. You are basically prepaying your own death benefit.

Example: Bob is 30 and buys a $1,000,000 permanent life insurance policy. At age 30, assume it only costs about $600 to insure him for $1,000,000 using a one-year term policy. But assume the annual premium for the permanent policy is $4,000. Why is Bob paying an extra $3,400 in the first year? Well, the insurance company is going to keep that $3,400 and credit it to his cash value within the insurance contract. This $3,400 is then invested for Bob and over time should grow. Every year as he contributes more money than the cost of insurance, his cash value is growing. It grows from the new premium payments, plus the interest rate or crediting rate that is being applied under the contract. As that cash grows, the amount of actual insurance he is buying declines.

By age 80, assume he has accumulated $800,000 of cash value in the contract from all those extra premium payments he made. Now he dies. Because it was a $1 million policy, his wife Danielle will get $1 million. But since he already had contributed an extra $800,000, the insurance company is only on the hook for $200,000. Thus, there is really only $200,000 of insurance in the policy.

This is how the insurance company reduces the costs of insurance as you get older with a permanent policy. If you live to 100, the cash value would be $1 million and the policy would generally "endow," meaning it matures and is paid to you. If you live long enough and buy a permanent policy, you will eventually prepay your own death benefit.

There can be a place for permanent life insurance, but it generally

| Age 65 & 80% Income Replacement | | | Mortgage Debt | Education Debt |
|---|---|---|---|---|
| Age | Capital to Income Ratio | Savings Ratio | Mortgage to Income Ratio | Debt to Avg. Income Ratio |
| 25 | 0.1 | 12% | 2.0 | 0.75 |
| 30 | 0.6 | 12% | 2.0 | 0.45 |
| 35 | 1.4 | 12% | 1.9 | 0.00 |
| 40 | 2.4 | 12% | 1.8 | |
| 45 | 3.7 | 15% | 1.7 | |
| 50 | 5.2 | 15% | 1.5 | |
| 55 | 7.1 | 15% | 1.2 | |
| 60 | 9.4 | 15% | 0.7 | |
| 65 | 12.0 | 15% | 0.0 | |

only makes sense for people with significant wealth or income. While this is a generalization, you probably need income of about $200,000 or assets above $1 million before a permanent policy would offer many benefits. There are certain tax and estate planning reasons that make permanent policies attractive, but again this is the exception, not the rule. If you are considering a permanent policy, work with a qualified financial and tax advisor to determine if the policy offers you some financial benefit.

The reason I spent that time explaining permanent insurance is because the insurance industry loves to sell it. The policies produce large profits for the insurance industry and agents. You will likely be asked about buying a permanent policy at some time, so you need to know whether it might fit your needs. The simple truth is this: for most people, term will do the trick. Let's add the Life Insurance Ratios to the Your Money Ratios chart:

| Investments | | Disability | Life Insurance |
|---|---|---|---|
| *Stocks* | *Bonds* | *% of Monthly Income* | *Insurance to Income Ratio* |
| 50% | 50% | .60 | 12 |
| 50% | 50% | .60 | 11.4 |
| 50% | 50% | .60 | 10.6 |
| 50% | 50% | .60 | 9.6 |
| 50% | 50% | .60 | 8.3 |
| 50% | 50% | .60 | 6.8 |
| 50% | 50% | .60 | 4.9 |
| 40% | 60% | .40 | 2.6 |
| 40% | 60% | .00 | 0 |

By following the ratios, you will be building sufficient capital for your retirement years, saving adequately each year, and systematically reducing your debt so that you will reach age 65 with no mortgage. You will also be investing your funds prudently, and protecting your income stream with disability insurance. You also have adequate life insurance to take care of the family should you die prematurely.

# 11

# The Long-Term Care Insurance Ratio

Finally, I bring you the least loved, least understood, but one of the most important type of insurance: Long-Term Care. Although it is the ugly stepchild of insurance, most people will need to consider getting long-term care. The economic cost of aging is the biggest risk to your financial security once you retire and are living off the earnings from your capital. This is why long-term care is an important aspect of your retirement planning.

> "Will buying long-term care insurance help move me from laborer to capitalist?"

Yes, if the projected income from your assets in retirement is not large enough to cover your potential long-term care costs for you and a spouse. Basically, long-term care costs are health-care costs that are not covered under your traditional health-care plan or under Medicare. Thus, it is an expense you would be forced to pay on your own if you needed the care. The expenses can be large, often in the hundreds of thousands of dollars, which can put a serious strain on your capital. The insurance can help protect your capital from being depleted to pay for significant health-care costs.

As with life and disability insurance, if you have enough capital, you may be able to cover the potential long-term care costs out of the income generated from your investments. This section will explain how to determine this. If your assets won't be large enough to do this, then you need to get the insurance to protect you from a sizable hit to your capital. Go back to our discussion about running your personal finances the way corporations run their finances: just as corporations plan many years in advance to cover the health-care needs of their retirees, you need to do the same. You will need to purchase long-term care insurance years before you retire. But first, I'd better explain the basics of long-term care so you understand how the ratio works.

## Long-Term Care Basics

Long-term care is health care that focuses on noncritical care. If you have a heart attack and go to the hospital, you will receive immediate treatment for the heart attack. This is critical or acute care and is covered by your health insurance or Medicare. But what if you had a stroke and lost the use of the left side of your body? You would have a hard time preparing meals, getting around, and bathing. You would need what is called long-term care, which would be assistance at home with these activities or admission into a facility where people can take care of these needs for you. Unfortunately, neither your health insurance policy nor Medicare pays for such services. You are on your own to cover these costs.

Technically, long-term care is triggered once you need help with at least two of the "activities of daily living," or ADLs: eating, bathing, dressing, toileting, transferring (moving back and forth), and continence. If you cannot perform at least two of these activities without substantial assistance, then you are generally considered in need of long-term care. Neither your health insurance nor Medicare will pay for this type of assistance beyond a short transition period after some form of acute treatment. For instance, Medicare covers about 3 months in a long-term care facility after a hospital stay. Once that is over, you are basically on your own.

Long-term care assistance may require you to have a health-care professional visit you each day at your home, to help you with the activities of daily living. Or you might not be in good enough health to live on your own and must be in some form of assisted-living facility or nursing home. These can cost between $3,000 and $7,000 a month, depending on the intensity of care you need. In 2009, the average cost for nursing home care was about $80,000 a year. That can be devastating to your capital.

Moreover, you can expect these costs to continue to rise rapidly. At just a 5% inflation rate, the $80,000 average cost goes to about $210,000 in 20 years. The cost of caring for us as we age is going up much faster than the rate of inflation for the rest of the economy, and you should expect it to do so for quite some time. At some point it will level off as health-care costs consume more of our income, but it may take many years and, at the end of the day, we may all end up spending a lot more of our income to care for ourselves as we age. But when you think about it, if you can't get around on your own, what else would you be spending money on? You might as well spend what you need to stay comfortable and improve your quality of life.

## Understanding Medicare

In addition to long-term care, it's important to understand how much it will cost for basic health coverage once you retire. The cost of health care will be one of your biggest challenges once you retire, and your assets need to be positioned to adequately fund these expenses. Many people have the misconception that "Medicare will take care of everything." But that's just not the case.

Health care is a unique expense because it basically costs the same for everyone. If you need heart surgery, the bill is the same whether you have $5,000,000 in assets or $500,000. This makes health care unlike the other spending decisions we make. For instance, if you want to buy a car, you can spend the $10,000 on a used Honda or $50,000 on the new Mercedes. This is a lifestyle choice and you have control over it. But not so with health care. You have little ability to reduce the costs should you need the care. Therefore, your assets need to be positioned to cover the costs.

Once you reach age 65, you will qualify for Medicare, a federally funded health-care program. You have been paying into it for your entire working career through the FICA tax system. A portion of your taxes is designated for the Medicare system. Medicare is good care, but it only covers a portion of your potential health-care costs. At age 65, you are eligible for what is called Medicare Part A, at no further cost. This covers most of your hospital expenses. Then you can buy Medicare Part B, which covers a portion of your doctor bills and other ancillary costs. You need both. At this time, the Medicare Part B premium costs about $100 to $150 a month, depending on your income. For a couple, plan on spending about $200 to $300 a month in Part B premiums in today's dollars.

Then you need Medicare Part D, which covers certain prescription drugs, but not all. This currently runs about $35 a person, or another $70 per couple. Thus, once retired, count on spending $300 to $500 per month as a couple to buy full Medicare coverage. That is about $4,000 to $6,000 a year. These costs will likely go up faster than the rate of inflation because the programs are underfunded. Expect that within 10 years, basic coverage may cost $6,000 or more per year for a married couple.

You may be wondering why I didn't cover Medicare Part C. Well, there is a Part C, but it has more to do with how Medicare Parts A and B are delivered in certain parts of the country.

On top of the premiums, you have to pay all your deductibles, coinsurance, and co-pays, which can easily run another couple thousand a year if you are on any medications or require any sort of ongoing care. When you add up the premiums and out-of-pocket expenses, it is likely that your health-care costs will be more than what the average retiree was spending on a mortgage prior to retiring. The average house in America costs about $200,000 a year, which is about a $1,200-a-month mortgage payment. In retirement, basic health-care costs can run at least $1,000 a month or more, particularly when we consider the premiums you may need to pay for long-term care.

Rising health-care costs are another reason to make sure you have your mortgage and other debts paid off before you retire. You will need to direct those mortgage payments to your health-care costs. If you carry a mortgage into retirement, you now need to add $1,000 a month of health-care costs on top of that. Understanding the potential costs of health-care in retirement will help keep you motivated to follow the ratios so that you enter retirement with a lot of assets and no debts. This gives you maximum flexibility to address health-care issues as they may arise.

Do not underestimate the costs of aging. They are one of the main reasons the Big Three automakers have been destroyed. The "legacy costs" for their retirees are enormous, and they don't have the funding to cover them. Detroit can go hat in hand to the government and plead for a bailout. You cannot. You can't afford to make the same mistakes they have. A good portion of the earnings from your assets will wind up dedicated toward staying healthy. What better use can you think of for your funds than staying healthy and improving your quality of life? Who cares if you have a nice house if you feel terrible or can't get the health care you need? It is a good use of your money. It will help you live a longer, healthier, and happier life. But you need the funding to pay for it.

## Medicaid Myths

Many people are under the impression that while Medicare doesn't cover the cost of long-term care, Medicaid will. Medicaid is a state-run health-care program that is funded half by the states and half by the federal government. You probably know someone who used Medicaid to pay for long-term care costs. Well, the first thing to understand about Medicaid is that it is a welfare program. Rules for eligibility differ by state, but they are all basically the same when it comes to your assets. *You can't have any.*

Essentially, you must deplete all your assets before you can qualify for Medicaid. Once you do qualify, then you must get care at a Medicaid facility, which may or may not be to your liking. You could opt to do this as long as you don't mind giving up control over the type of care and facility you will be in. This means, though, that if you happen to recover and then leave a facility, you have no assets left to live on. That could be a problem. Or, the government could change the Medicaid rules—you never know what sort of care you might qualify for. Also, if you wanted to pass along any assets to children or grandchildren, there would be nothing left. There are all sorts of reasons why relying on Medicaid is a bad idea for anyone who wants any sort of control over how or whether they will be cared for.

When I say you can't have any assets, I mean *no* assets. In most states, you can't have a net worth of more than a few thousand dollars. This means no car, no savings account, nada. Once you go into a facility under Medicaid, all of your earnings (such as Social Security) go to the facility, except a small stipend (usually less than $100 a month) for personal care expenses. This means you won't be going out to lunch, buying clothes, giving gifts, or having any semblance of financial independence. The system will basically house and care for you, and that's all you have. It is not a pretty picture.

An even bigger problem with Medicaid eligibility arises if you are married and either one or both spouses needs long-term care. Let's say that you are married, have $800,000 in assets, and your spouse needs long-term care that costs $80,000 a year. Medicaid will not pick up the tab for your spouse until you spend down your $800,000 to about $100,000. That is about all the Medicare rules allow the healthy spouse to keep. This means the healthy spouse will be effectively bankrupt, but the unhealthy spouse will now qualify for Medicaid. I don't think this is the type of situation you want to find yourself in. When long-term care costs appear, it is a terribly stressful time in your life. You are likely dealing with the decline of your spouse, perhaps their permanent incapacity, and harbingers of their death. You don't want to be worried about losing your house or paying for your own meals down the road during such difficult times.

> Medicaid rules are highly complex and vary by state. The general framework requires you to spend all of your assets prior to qualifying for care. And if you have a spouse, the spouse generally must spend down most of your joint assets.

## Buying Long-Term Care Insurance

So, if you cannot rely on your health insurance or government programs to cover long-term care, what can you do? First, you need to determine how much long-term care expense you could afford to fund yourself in retirement. Then, if you cannot cover the full cost out of your investment assets, you should consider getting a long-term care policy.

Long-term care policies are similar to disability policies in that the benefits are triggered by some form of physical disability. But long-term care policies are tied to the cost of care, not to wage replacement. So, they each cover a different type of risk. While working you need disability insurance to cover your wages. Once retired, you need to protect your capital against potentially ruinous health-care costs.

There is, however, a transition period prior to age 65 where it may make sense to drop your disability insurance and pick up long-term care insurance. Also, some insurers are coming out with disability policies that allow you to convert them to long-term care once retired. This type of policy makes the most sense, and we are likely to see more of them in the future. But, for now, the conversion benefits are not that strong and these policies are in their infancy. Under current market conditions, you will need disability insurance while working, and you may need to consider long-term care insurance, once retired, if your assets are not large enough to cover the potential costs for you and your spouse. I'll talk more about these options a little later.

Long-term care policies are priced in the form of a daily benefit and a term of years. You have to choose both when buying a policy. The daily benefit generally ranges from about $50 a day to over $500. In terms of an annual benefit, that is about $20,000 for the $50-a-day policy to over $180,000 a year for the $500 daily benefit. Thus, there is usually a benefit amount to fit your needs. The higher the daily benefit, the higher the premium. You also need to select a term of years for how long the benefits will be paid. Coverage ranges from as short as two years all the way up to a lifetime benefit (meaning the policy pays for as long as you live). The longer the benefit period, the higher the premium.

Most policies also have an inflation adjustment option, in which the daily benefit is increased each year by an inflation factor. Generally, the policies allow for a 5% inflation cap each year. It is important to get an inflation feature with any long-term care policy you buy. While the inflation adjuster will help, it won't, however, keep up with the entire increase in the cost of long-term care. There isn't much you can do about that. For the time being, the cost of care is rising faster than 5% a year. It won't continue forever; eventually, the market will be forced to become more efficient. But for the next 20 years, assume long-term care costs will increase faster than inflation.

You will also need to choose a waiting period before the policy kicks in. This is the time period during which you would cover the costs of long-term care before you could apply for insurance benefits. Waiting periods go from as short as 90 days up to as long as one year. As we have discussed before, the less exposure an insurance company has, the lower the premium is. Because you only want to use the insurance to cover costs you cannot handle yourself, it generally makes sense to use a longer waiting period. This will lower the cost of your premium, which is important because the premium just reduces your income each year during your retirement. Plus, it is possible you may not need any long-term care, so why pay the extra premium? In general, you should consider policies with at least a six-month wait and even up to one year. If you have been following my ratios, you should be able to cover up to a year's worth of expenses without putting a huge strain on your budget.

> Example: You buy a policy with a $120 daily benefit, a 5%
> inflation rider, a one-year waiting period, and a benefit period
> of 10 years. That means you are entitled to about $43,000 of
> insurance benefits each year and the $43,000 increases at 5%
> a year. If you eventually need care, you must cover the first
> year's worth of expenses. Then, once the year passes, the policy
> would pay for 10 years.

So, how much long-term care could you afford to pay for once you're retired? When it comes to insurance, you should always look at insuring the event that will really cause you financial stress. Many people could probably afford to pay the $30,000 to $70,000 that one year of care might cost. About 80% of the people who need long-term care need it for less than three years. Usually, people need long-term care after a serious illness or injury. They are in a situation of declining health and can't take care of themselves. Many pass away from the illness or injury. Thus, the long-term care is often the last stop on the continuum of care.

For three years of care costing $80,000 a year, you would need $240,000 to cover the expense. If you are married, double that to about $500,000, in today's dollars. Thus, if you have $500,000 in assets, it appears as if you probably could self-insure. While this looks like a good plan, it probably won't work very well to address long-term care. The reason is that your biggest risk from long-term care is not a one- or two-year stay in a facility. At $80,000 a year, your retirement savings or the equity in your home could probably easily cover several years of care at the end of your life. The real risk is a much longer period of care for one or both spouses. This is where your financial security could be challenged. Stays of 5 to 10 years are rare today, but may become much more common in the future. You just don't know; there are no meaningful statistics to help assess the risk. Today's stats will change as we figure out how to age better and live longer. Thus, you may see many more people needing assisted-living or facilities-based long-term care in the future.

The goal is to insure against a sustained period of long-term care assistance—longer than four years, due to diseases like Alzheimer's and Parkinson's disease, or a disability caused by a stroke or an illness such as MS. These are the situations where you can find yourself or your spouse needing 5 to 10 or more years of intensive assistance. This is the type of health-care expense that will threaten your capital.

## Calculating Your Long-Term Care Exposure

If you are single, the formula for determining how much care you can pay for is easy. You have three potential sources: Social Security, any pension income, and the income from your retirement savings. To estimate the income from your savings, use the 5% distribution rule. If the three income sources add up to about $80,000 in today's dollars, then you can afford to self-insure the cost of care. If they add up to less than $80,000, then the difference between the $80,000 of care and your estimated income is the gap that you should consider having covered by a long-term care policy. Here is the formula:

(Investments × 5%) + Social Security + Pension Income
  − $80,000
= Estimated Long-Term Care Insurance Need

Example: Assume you retire today with $800,000 of assets, have Social Security of $18,000 a year, but have no pension. At a 5% distribution from your savings, you can antici-pate $40,000 a year of income from your investments, plus $18,000 from Social Security, for a total of $58,000. Sub-tract $58,000 from $80,000, and you only have a gap of about $22,000 a year. Thus, you should consider buying a long-term care policy that provides at least $22,000 of inflation-adjusted care. With the long-term care insurance coupled with your estimated income from your investments and Social Security, you can be quite confident you could pay for all of the long-term care you would need for as long as you need it.

This formula gives you a margin of error if long-term care costs rise more rapidly than you thought, in which case your income plus the insurance would not be enough to fully pay for your care. Let's assume the same numbers in the above example, but it turns out that the cost of long-term care is higher than you anticipated. In addition to the income from your investments and your Social Security, you have to liquidate $20,000 a year in assets to pay for the care. Thus, your $800,000 of assets would be slowly declining, as would be your annual income in the future. But, it would likely take you 20 years before you would deplete the money, which should be enough of a safety net.

If you are married, the formula is the same, except you double everything. To be safe, you need to assume that both of you may need care some day. That means $160,000 for two. We estimate your annual household income, add up your Social Security, any pension income, and the projected income from your savings. If that income adds up to $160,000, then you are in a position to self-insure. If not, then subtract your income from $160,000 to determine the gap that you should consider covering with long-term care insurance.

But with couples, we have to split the gap for each spouse, and then purchase a long-term care policy for each spouse equal to half of the gap. This is because we cannot be sure which spouse might need the care. If you only buy insurance on one of you and it is the other who goes into a facility, the insurance is of no value.

Example: Assume you have $1.5 million in assets, $25,000 in total Social Security, and no pension. Using the 5% distribution rule plus $25,000 from Social Security, we figure your total household income to be $100,000. This is less than the $160,000 estimated cost of care, so you will need to cover about $60,000 with insurance. Since there are two of you, split the $60,000 and each of you should get an inflation-adjusted long-term care policy for $30,000 a year.

A few years go by and you need long-term care at $80,000 a year, but your spouse does not. You can take one half of the household retirement income ($50,000) and dedicate that toward paying the long-term care costs. Then, with your $30,000 of long-term care insurance, you are fully covered for the long-term care expenses. This allows the healthy spouse to retain all of the household investments and continue to live off half of the household income. In theory, you could continue with this situation for an indefinite period of time. If the second spouse subsequently needs care, the other $50,000 of income can be used along with his or her $30,000 long-term care policy—and you still have about $1,500,000 of assets to cover any potential shortfalls or increasing costs.

Here is the formula:

(Investments × 5%) + Social Security + Pension Benefits
   − $160,000
= Estimated Long-Term Care Need
Long-Term Care Need / 2 = Amount Per Spouse

## Getting Only the Coverage You Need

You should start looking into long-term care in your mid 50s. At that age, you should still be healthy enough to get coverage. It is also at a point in your life when your assets and income should be high enough to help support paying for the premiums. There is an argument to be made that once you reach your late 50s, you could consider dropping your disability insurance and just getting the long-term care. Because disability only pays until age 65, your benefit period is getting pretty short in your late 50s. But, this should only be done on a case-by-case basis. You may need to carry both types of policies for a few years, because more of your income will need to be dedicated to health-care needs as you age.

It is difficult to qualify for long-term care insurance, so the earlier you can apply, the better. Many people are declined because they already have some form of a serious health issue. Remember, insurers don't like sick people. So, the earlier you apply, the better.

If you are going to buy a policy prior to your retirement, you will need to project the value of your retirement assets to get an estimate of your potential income. You will also need to make some projections about any pensions and Social Security. Then you need to estimate the long-term care costs by taking today's costs and projecting them out from your retirement age. I suggest having a financial professional help you with this.

Long-term care benefits are generally not subject to income tax. Thus, the full amount of the annual insurance benefit is there to pay for your care. Plus, if you are taking distributions from your IRAs or selling investments to pay for care, you will get a deduction for the cost of the care to help lower the tax bite. The rule is that if your health-care costs exceed 7.5% of your Adjusted Gross Income, then you can deduct the costs above that amount. The ability to deduct the costs will effectively lower or almost eliminate your tax bill for the funds you spend on long-term care. This makes it easier to pay for long-term care because you don't have to pay Uncle Sam at the same time.

How long a benefit period should you purchase? Policies generally run from as short as two years up to a lifetime. Usually, insurers provide for a choice of years of coverage spanning two, three, four, six, and ten years, or lifetime benefits. When you get your quotes for long-term care coverage, your agent will give you quotes for each of the available terms. The premium goes up for longer terms.

So, let's assume you run my formulas and you determine you need $40,000 of coverage per spouse. You get a quote for a $40,000-a-year policy with a lifetime benefit period, and the premium is $3,000 per year per spouse. If you can afford it, then this is your safest bet. You will have full coverage for as long as you may need it. You don't have to try to guess how many years of care you might use. But many people cannot afford the lifetime benefit to cover them for the full amount of their exposure. Assume we have a couple that can only afford to spend $4,500 a year on long-term care, which would be $2,250 per spouse. When they get their long-term care quotes, they may find that for $4,500 they can get either a $40,000 three-year policy for each spouse, or a $30,000 ten-year policy for each spouse.

Remember the concept of insurance: to cover liabilities that would otherwise result in a financial disaster. You only want to use it for expenses you cannot cover yourself. As I mentioned previously, the biggest risk to your financial security is an extended period of long-term care expenses, something beyond four years. So, if your choice is between a shorter period with a higher benefit or a longer period with a lower benefit, you should generally go with the longer period and lower benefit amount.

Let's say you end up needing care for eight years. With the $40,000 policy, you are on your own after four years and have to cover the entire $80,000 a year for years five through eight. With the 10-year policy, you have $10,000 less in coverage every year, but you get it for the full eight years. You have total coverage of $240,000 ($30,000 for eight years) versus $160,000 ($40,000 for four years). Thus, the longer-term policy provides a better hedge against your biggest risk.

There are some new insurance policies that give couples a pool of money to use instead of an annual benefit amount. For instance, they may provide you with $1 million of coverage for your long-term care expenses. Either spouse may access the benefit pool. In many ways, this makes the process simpler because you don't know which spouse might need care or for how long. These are newer policy provisions but they are an interesting option. Again, in these circumstances, focus on getting the largest benefit pool that you can for the longest time period.

Here is a chart to help you organize the issues of long-term care planning:

| *Single* | | | | | |
|---|---|---|---|---|---|
| Determine the current cost of LTC. | Determine your total retirement income. | If the cost of LTC is higher than your income, this is your insurance gap. | Get LTC coverage for the gap. | If you can afford a lifetime benefit, get it. | If not, then seek to get the longest benefit period you can afford. |
| *Married* | | | | | |
| Determine the current cost of LTC, and double it for both spouses. | Determine your total retirement income. | If the cost of LTC is higher than your income, this is your insurance gap. | Divide the gap by 2 and get a LTC policy for each spouse equal to that amount. | If you can afford a lifetime benefit for both spouses, get it. | If not, then seek to get the longest benefit period you can afford. |

## The Long-Term Care Ratio

The Long-Term Care Ratio is based on the ability of your invest-ment income to cover the expenses of long-term care. The ratio is calculated by taking your projected retirement income and divid-ing it by the projected annual cost of long-term care (LTC for con-venience). If the ratio is less than one, then you have a gap and need coverage. If the ratio is over one, then your retirement income should be able to fully cover the cost of care and you don't need the insurance.

Example: Assume LTC costs $80,000 a year and you are mar-ried. Your projected LTC costs are $160,000 a year. Assume

the income from your investments and Social Security is
$130,000 a year. The ratio equals your retirement income
divided by your LTC costs—$130,000 / $160,000 = .81. This
means your income will cover about 80% of your projected
LTC costs, so you have a gap of 20%, which needs to be covered by insurance.

I have added the LTC Ratio to my ratios chart starting at age
55, which is when you should start looking at long-term care
insurance:

| Age 65 & 80% Income Replacement | | | Mortgage Debt | Education Debt |
| --- | --- | --- | --- | --- |
| *Age* | *Capital to Income Ratio* | *Savings Ratio* | *Mortgage to Income Ratio* | *Debt to Avg. Income Ratio* |
| 25 | 0.1 | 12% | 2.0 | 0.75 |
| 30 | 0.6 | 12% | 2.0 | 0.45 |
| 35 | 1.4 | 12% | 1.9 | 0.00 |
| 40 | 2.4 | 12% | 1.8 | |
| 45 | 3.7 | 15% | 1.7 | |
| 50 | 5.2 | 15% | 1.5 | |
| 55 | 7.1 | 15% | 1.2 | |
| 60 | 9.4 | 15% | 0.7 | |
| 65 | 12.0 | 15% | 0.0 | |

Long-term care is an evolving industry. New policy provisions and benefit structures will continue to be rolled out to try to meet the needs of baby boomers as they age. While the structures may change, the formula for determining your exposure stays the same. Figure out how much of the anticipated annual cost you can cover from your income sources, and if this is less than the annual estimated cost of long-term care, get a policy to cover that gap. If you cannot afford a lifetime policy for the entire gap amount, get the most coverage for the longest period you can afford. Or, if you have access to a pool of funds for both spouses, focus on getting access to the biggest pool of benefits for the longest period.

| Investments | | Disability | Life Insurance | LTC Ratio |
|---|---|---|---|---|
| *Stocks* | *Bonds* | *% of Monthly Income* | *Insurance to Income Ratio* | *Projected Retirement Income to LTC Costs* |
| 50% | 50% | .60 | 12 | x |
| 50% | 50% | .60 | 11.4 | x |
| 50% | 50% | .60 | 10.6 | x |
| 50% | 50% | .60 | 9.6 | x |
| 50% | 50% | .60 | 8.3 | x |
| 50% | 50% | .60 | 6.8 | x |
| 50% | 50% | .60 | 4.9 | = or > 1 |
| 40% | 60% | .40 | 2.6 | = or > 1 |
| 40% | 60% | .00 | 0 | = or > 1 |

It is also likely that your long-term care premium will increase over time. With luck, any increases will be modest. Many insurance carriers have underpriced the cost of these policies because they were not able to accurately estimate how many people might need care. Basically, more people needed care than they thought and it costs more than they thought. They have learned from these mistakes, but estimating the costs is a tough business, so expect that future mistakes will be made.

When selecting long-term care, be especially careful about the insurance carrier you choose. You want to investigate any history they have had of premium increases and also pay close attention to their credit rating. You want an insurer with a very high credit rating so that odds are they will be around to pay your claims when needed. That's especially true in these tumultuous financial times, when the survival of even giant international insurers is in question. Also be careful about going with an insurer whose premiums appear much lower than everyone else. You may end up paying more later.

The reason I have spent so much time on long-term care is so that you realize how important funding your health-care needs will be in retirement. Staying physically and mentally healthy, and having the assets to care for yourself, should be a major focus of your retirement years. I'm going to talk about this more in the "Health Insurance" chapter, so let's go there next.

# 12

# Health Insurance

Will health insurance help move you from being a laborer to a capitalist? Yes, because for several thousand dollars a year you can insure against a potential financial disaster. The fact remains that the National Coalition on Health Care found that 50% of all personal bankruptcy filings are the result of excessive health-care costs. Health insurance has the potential to impact your journey from laborer to capitalist more than any other type of insurance. Having it frees up other capital to be invested and also protects your savings from being wiped out by a medical illness or injury.

As you know, Congress enacted major health-care legislation in 2010. While the legislation was called health-care "reform," it left the current system basically intact. For the next several years, not much will change with your health insurance if you currently obtain it through your employer. You'll need to make the same risk/reward analysis with your plans as you were doing before. The relevant questions are outlined in this chapter.

For those who were uninsurable, however, the 2010 law will make a difference. States will have to set up insurance exchanges to allow individuals with preexisting conditions to buy a basic health care plan. And depending on how much income you make, you may be entitled to subsidies from the federal government to help you and your family afford the plan. While this is of course an important change, especially for those who were uninsurable, the basic cost and coverage structure for health care will continue for many years. Expect to see more battles on this front, with the laws and coverage rules changing as the political winds change.

## Health Insurance Basics

You may be wondering why there is no Health Insurance Ratio. The answer is simple: the amount of health coverage you should carry doesn't depend on your income. You should get the best coverage you can get for a cost you can afford until the time you're eligible for Medicare. It's that simple. The best coverage is whatever balances access to quality care, affordability, comprehensive benefits, and good customer service.

I won't spend a lot of time on health insurance because you already know that you have to get it and keep it. But I will spend time covering a few of the basics. You will need to know these things because you will be required to make choices about how to handle your health insurance. In the past, this information would have been irrelevant to most people, because the vast majority of Americans got their health coverage from their employers. Most still do, but the percentage is dropping. An estimated 46 million Americans lack any health insurance, and that was before the recession. As the government continues to work on new solutions, it is likely you will have to make more of your own health-care purchasing decisions. If you end up buying your own coverage from the private market, it will be one of the larger bills you will pay each month, and could affect your ability to move from laborer to capitalist. Bottom line, the less you can spend on health care, while still getting quality care, the more you will have available for savings. So the goal is to try to spend less but still get access to the care you need.

There are three basic types of health insurance policies: traditional indemnity policies, preferred provider networks, and health maintenance organizations. The difference among the policies comes down to how much control the insurer has over your care and how much of the costs of care you are willing to bear. The three choices are as follows:

- An indemnity policy is one where the insurance company basically pays whatever costs you incur. The insurer has no oversight or control over the services you select. They essentially have to pay your health-care bills. This, of course, is a very expensive type of insurance and not offered very much anymore. But it was the original type of health insurance. Because there was really no way to control costs, indemnity policies helped contribute to the rising cost of health care, which is why you don't see them much anymore.

- A preferred provider organization, or PPO, is the most common type of health plan being used today. It is basically a network of physicians and hospitals that have signed a contract with your health insurer. These health-care providers agree to discounted fee schedules to be a part of the insurer's network. These discounts help reduce the costs of health care. If you enroll in a PPO plan, you incur lower health-care bills in the form of deductibles and co-payments if you use one of the physicians or hospitals

in your network. They are generally pretty flexible, but
they are more restrictive than an indemnity plan, and thus
are less expensive. You can often use health-care providers
that are not part of the PPO network, but your costs go
up. Thus, the financial incentive is to use those within the
network.

- Finally, we have the health maintenance organization, or
  HMO. An HMO is a type of health insurance where the
  insurer has a great deal of control over who you see and
  what services you get. The HMO hires an exclusive network of doctors and hospitals who agree to provide care
  to the HMO's members. Generally, you have little to no
  flexibility to go outside of this network—it is a closed system. Also, the insurer has many restrictions on how you
  can access care and the level of care that your physician can
  prescribe. This level of control helps them reduce costs, but
  it often can create a very frustrating situation for you, the
  patient. Because it is more restrictive, the premiums are
  generally lower.

Since most people still get their health insurance from their employer,
you will need to select one of the plans your employer offers. Generally, you won't have access to an indemnity plan anymore. The
choices are usually between some form of PPO or an HMO. To
understand how to make the choice, you have to understand the
basic costs associated with a health-care plan. There are usually four
levels of fees and they are different depending on the type of plan
you choose. You generally have a premium payment, coinsurance
payment, co-payments, and an annual deductible:

- The premium is the monthly amount you pay for your
  health plan. Many employers require employees to share in
  some portion of the monthly premium. It can vary from

as low as 10% to 50% or more. Essentially, employers
will pick up more of the tab if you select a plan that has
less generous benefits. That is because the plan with the less
generous benefits costs less. Since the employer is paying
most of the bill, they want to encourage employees to
choose less elaborate plans. To do so, they will often cover
a larger percentage of the monthly premium. In many cases,
a less generous plan may fit your needs. This is usually the
case if you are basically healthy.

The deductible is the amount of money you must pay annually
before the insurance company starts to pay anything. The higher the
deductible, the lower the monthly premium is. This is how insurance works. If you are willing to bear more of the costs, then the
insurer's exposure is lower. Thus, it can charge a lower premium for
the policy. Deductibles can range from as low as $250 to as high as
$5,000 under some plans.

Example: Assume you have a plan with a $1,000 deductible.
The insurance company doesn't begin to pay any bills until you
incur and pay the first $1,000 of costs. Because most people
don't get really sick each year, if you have a high-deductible
plan, the insurer doesn't usually have to pay out much in benefits each year. Thus, it can charge less for the policy. If there was
no deductible at all, then the insurer is on the hook for the first
dollar you spend. You have no disincentive to spend on health
care, which means the risk that you will run to the doctor
for even the smallest problem is higher. Thus, companies will
charge more because they know you will probably have some
routine care each year and they will have to pay for it.

- Coinsurance is the percentage of each medical bill that
  you are required to pay when you receive services. Often

the percentage is 20%. The coinsurance does not kick in until you have met your deductible. Once you meet your deductible, you will still be paying 20% of the bills, but the insurer steps in to cover the other 80%. This makes people think twice about getting care because they have to foot some of the bill. In a PPO, the coinsurance amount often goes up if you go out of network. You may pay 30% of the bill instead of 20%. That way you can decide whether the specific doctor's skills are worth the extra expense.

- The co-payment is the charge you have to pay when you get certain standard services. For instance, when you have a doctor's visit, there is generally a co-payment of $10 or $20. Or, if you have prescriptions, you often have a co-payment. In the case of prescriptions, the co-payment is usually less if you use generic drugs. Again, these payments are designed to get you to think about the cost of health care and try to choose the lower-cost option if medically appropriate. The co-payment is usually not counted as part of your deductible.

So before the insurer will pay anything, you generally have to hit your annual deductible each year. Once you do that, the insurer will begin to pay bills in accordance with the coinsurance formula. Often this is an 80/20 split. This means you are still incurring 20% of the costs. But most policies have a maximum out-of-pocket cost that you would be required to cover each year. If you got really sick and needed $200,000 of care, it wouldn't make sense for you to have to pay $40,000 for the care. That defeats the purpose of the insurance. So, you have coinsurance up to a certain point. Generally, it is somewhere between $5,000 and $10,000 a year, which means that no matter how sick you get, you won't have to pay more than the maximum out of pocket in a calendar year.

## Encouraging Responsibility

When you compare health plans, you will notice that the differences are generally based on how these four payments are arranged. If you choose a plan where you bear more of the risks for basic care, then the annual premium is generally lower. Since you are probably required to pay a percentage of the monthly premium, choosing the lower-cost plan can save you money each month. But, if you get sick, you pay a bigger part of the initial bills. That is the trade-off. If you choose a plan with a low deductible, low coinsurance, and low co-payment features, then the monthly premium is generally a lot higher. By varying the plan features, employees are given some choices as to which risks they want to bear.

Understand that there is a fine balance to be struck between encouraging you to make responsible health-care choices and discouraging you from seeking medical care at all. What health insurers want is to structure their programs so that people will have access to basic medical care that keeps them well, thereby reducing costs for major medical procedures. At the same time, they want enough potential costs to be borne by the consumer that people are discouraged from seeking health care frivolously, such as going to the emergency room when their child wakes up with a fever that could easily be brought down with over-the-counter medication.

One of the factors often blamed for the rising cost of health care in this country is the fact that Americans have easy access to a broad range of covered medical care, and are not shy about using it even for the smallest problems. We also tend to live lifestyles that contribute to health problems and rely on doctors to "fix" them. Thus, we tend to run to the health-care system more often than we should—certainly more often than Europeans, who typically have less access to elective care but near-universal access to essential medical care and have lower mortality rates and higher life expectancy as a result. I suspect that one part of a future health-care solution will ask Americans to bear a greater portion of the cost (or the risk) of nonessential medical care while encouraging us to live more responsibly and focus on preventing illness.

I have already talked about the fact that health care will become a larger and larger portion of your overall costs as you age, and how important it is to retire with no debt so you can devote more of your capital to health-care costs. But the core message is even simpler: staying healthy as you age means money in your pocket and a better quality of life in every way. Thus, doing everything you can to remain healthy as you get into your 50s, 60s, and beyond is actually an investment in a long and successful retirement.

Consider the difference between two 70-year-old male retirees: Retiree #1, who is overweight and sedentary, and Retiree #2, who has exercised vigorously and eaten a healthy diet since he was in his 30s. Retiree #1 is far more likely to suffer from heart disease, diabetes, arthritis, and other health problems, so he is more likely to incur costs that are not covered by Medicare, particularly for medication. He is far more likely to need long-term care in the future, which, unless he has insurance, could deplete his capital quickly. If a financial crisis were to arise, he would probably be unable to work to earn emergency income. And his quality of life is probably poor because his mobility is restricted, he has less energy, and spends a great deal of time seeing doctors.

Retiree #2 has been working on preventing disease and staying healthy for decades. He's active and fit and sees his doctor once a year for a physical and the usual screenings. He takes little or no medication, so his medical costs are all covered by Medicare. If things got really tight, he has the energy to go out and get a job. And he's got a great quality of life because his health lets him do pretty much whatever he wants. Isn't that what retirement is supposed to be about?

The difference is that one retiree has unfortunately neglected his health, while the other has taken responsibility for it. The difference can be thousands of dollars in additional costs and even lost income over a 25-year retirement (assuming Retiree #1 lasts that long). The bottom line is that, in the future, with health care changing, smart consumers must start taking greater responsibility for preventing illness and maintaining good health as they enter their retirement years. I don't have a crystal ball, but I think it is likely that future health care will reward people who focus on wellness and preventive care while financially penalizing those who neglect their health. We may have had the luxury of operating that way in the past, but no more.

Since aging and health problems go hand in hand, it is in your financial, medical, and lifestyle interests to focus much of your energy—both before and in retirement—on living a healthy, fit lifestyle. Doing so will reduce your insurance premiums and medical care costs, preserve more of your capital, allow you to return to work if you want to or need to, and give you the best quality of life possible.

## How to Buy Health Insurance

As with all insurance, there are two payment risks you must manage. The first is the monthly premium, which is fixed and which you must pay whether or not you get sick. The second is the out-of-pocket costs you must pay if you do get sick, which you often cannot predict. So, in most cases, it makes sense to lower the cost of the monthly premium you know you must pay, and increase your exposure on the out-of-pocket costs you don't know whether you will need to pay.

That way, if you take good care of yourself and don't get very sick, you will generally end up better off financially by using a policy that has the lower premium because you are taking on the risk of paying more of the initial costs. If you do get sick, then you at least know your maximum exposure based on the deductible and maximum out-of-pocket costs. Since it is unlikely you will get really sick each year, you may lose out in a few years, but over your lifetime you will probably do better by being willing to take on the higher deductibles and costs.

If you are already sick or have a chronic illness that requires consistent care, you are in a different situation. You basically know you will pay your deductible and will quickly be paying the coinsurance amount. The savings in monthly premiums probably are not enough to offset the higher out-of-pocket costs you will be paying, especially if you think you will be paying them every year. Thus, you may want to consider a higher premium plan with the lower out-of-pocket costs.

One new type of health-care plan has been around for a few years and is gaining popularity. It is called a High Deductible Health Plan, or HDHP. The theory behind the HDHP is that you take out a health-care policy with a high annual deductible, say $2,500. Because you are willing to pay the first $2,500 of costs you incur, your insurance premium is much lower as the insurance company is now on the hook only for larger health-care bills, which are less likely to occur. You can use the money you are saving in lower monthly premiums to build an account to pay for any large health-care bills later on.

There is legislation that defines what constitutes an HDHP, and sets forth the minimum deductibles for individual and family coverage. Deductibles can be higher than these minimum figures, and each health plan is a little bit different.

> Example: Assume you elect an HDHP plan with a $2,500 deductible. This plan costs $200 less a month in premiums than the PPO plan with the $500 deductible. So, you choose the HDHP and then direct your $200 into a savings account to be used for your future health-care costs. If you don't get sick this year, you have saved $2,400 in your savings account.

If you don't get sick next year, then you have $4,800 in the account. This money can then be used to pay for your future health-care deductibles and coinsurance fees. In the third year you get sick and incur $1,500 in costs. You pay the $1,500 out of your savings account and still have $3,300 left. If you can do this for many years in a row, you can begin to build a sizable savings account to manage your future health-care costs.

## Health Savings Accounts

To provide an incentive to do this, Congress allows individuals who have HDHP plans to open what are called Health Savings Accounts (HSAs). You can fund an HSA up to the amount of your annual deductible. In the above example, that would be $2,400 a year. Plus, you get a tax deduction for the contribution into the HSA, similar to your 401(k) Plan. Then, if you need to use the money, you get to take the money out tax-free. This is a big benefit and can greatly reduce the overall costs of health care for you. If you could fund an HSA for 15 or 20 years, you could conceivably build an account worth $50,000 for your retiree health-care costs.

Money that you put into an HSA will continue to grow tax-deferred throughout your retirement years. This is another benefit of taking care of your health: if you don't have to tap your HSA funds, you can accrue more. Then, if you take the funds out to pay for medical expenses, the distributions are still tax-free. This means you can use the funds to pay for health-care costs Medicare does not cover. A well-funded HSA could be a very valuable asset for your retirement.

They are interesting plans, and if you have an employer who offers an HDHP, you should consider experimenting with it. They work best for people who are basically healthy. If you are sick and run through several thousand dollars a year in health-care costs, you may find that you don't really get ahead for taking the added risk of the high deductible. So, again, you may be better with a traditional PPO or HMO plan.

There are a number of technical requirements that go along with an HDHP plan, but if your employer offers one, your human resources department will be up to speed on all of this. They can help you evaluate the plan and figure out how to open up an HSA and begin funding it.

## Using Your Human Resources Department

The HR department can also help you sort through the various PPO and HMO options they may offer. Again, your basic choice is between a lower monthly premium but a higher annual out-of-pocket cost if you or a family member gets sick, or a higher monthly premium but a lower out-of-pocket cost if you or a family member gets sick. Each employer will have variations on this theme, but that is fundamentally how the health-insurance market currently operates.

With an understanding of the basic risk-management issues and the four levels of fees, you should be in a good position to make an informed choice given your health status. Many people often forget to take advantage of all the help that is available from their human resources departments. They are there to make your life easier and generally really want to help employees maximize their benefits packages. Take the time to visit. I think it will pay off handsomely for you.

If your company does not offer an HSA, it may offer what is called a flexible spending account (FSA), or sometimes also called a "cafeteria plan." This is an account that you can put money into each year to pay your anticipated health-care costs that are not covered by insurance, such as co-payments and deductibles, and dental and vision expenses. The trick is that you cannot roll the unused money over from year to year. This means you have to guess how much you might use for the year and put that into the FSA. You get a tax deduction for the money that goes into the FSA, and any funds that are used to pay health-care costs are not subject to income tax. This is similar to the HSA account, but the major difference is that you cannot build up a balance from year to year in an FSA.

> Example: Assume you have an FSA at work that allows you to make contributions to pay for your anticipated medical expenses for the year. You decide to put $100 a month into the plan, which is $1,200 for the year. You go to the dentist and get a bill for $600. You submit the bill to your FSA administrator, who will distribute $600 from your account tax-free. Those funds are used to pay the dental bill. This is a lot more cost-effective than paying the dentist with after-tax dollars. Assuming you are taxed at 25%, if you cannot deduct the $600, it costs you an extra $150 in taxes. Therefore, the dentist really costs you about $750 if you can't deduct the expense. Now you can see why using an FSA makes sense.

If you have an FSA, consider funding it. Your human resources department can help you figure out how to fund it and then how to access the funds to pay your bills. Many FSAs now have debit cards or other user-friendly features that make them convenient. Even if not convenient, it is worth the tax savings to open one. But remember not to overfund it, because you cannot use the money next year. If you put in $1,000 and only spend $700, your employer keeps the other $300. You forfeit it. This is why it is a good idea to check on your FSA balance in September of each year to see how much is left.

Then get whatever dental, vision, or other discretionary care scheduled before the end of the year. This way you will at least use all your FSA for health-care costs you were going to incur anyway.

## Final Tips

With the health-care legislation that was passed in 2010, it should be easier for individuals to find coverage if they cannot obtain it through their employers. That is a very important change. The old system was simply unfair for those who were caught between jobs or left without coverage because of circumstances outside their control.

Most of us will continue to have health care through our employers under a group plan. And we'll still need to decide whether we want a PPO or HMO plan, and how much of a deductible or co-payment arrangement we can afford. The basic tradeoff between lower premiums and higher out-of-pocket costs will continue to exist.

Since health-care coverage is likely to generate much debate, it's important to stay informed about changes to the system and how they will affect your planning. For instance, if you intend to retire before you're eligible for Medicare, you need to think very carefully about how you will access care and what level of coverage you can afford. Even though the new insurance exchanges may help individuals with coverage, it could still be costly. And remember, Congress can always change the rules.

# 13

# Getting Professional Help

The title of this chapter is a deliberate pun, because I may have given you so much information about investing and retirement that you feel like you're in need of the services of a good therapist. While that may be the case, that's not the kind of professional help I'm talking about. It's vital that, just as you seek the experience and expertise of a physician when dealing with your health, and an attorney when dealing with legal matters, you seek the assistance of a trained, experienced financial advisor to help you make wise, sound, rational decisions in the incredibly complex financial world.

While you now have tremendous knowledge about how to manage your personal finances, the material in this book does not substitute for individual advice. I never intended it to. The book provides you with an overarching philosophy for how to manage personal finances, but most people could benefit from individual advice and guidance. Therefore, it is generally a prudent idea to get some professional assistance. The good news is that there are many qualified and ethical advisors out there who are in a position to help.

Financial advice is scalable, meaning that similar advice can often be provided to many different people at the same time. Because of this, you can generally get access to quality advice for a reasonable fee. For instance, if an advisor develops an investment management strategy, he can use the same or similar strategy for each client. Thus, no single client has to bear the full cost of creating and implementing the strategy. This makes the advice more affordable for the average client.

While there is a lot of free information out there in the financial media, it doesn't constitute advice. Advice comes through a relationship that you establish with an advisor who knows your individual circumstances and is committed to helping you reach your individual goals. Anything else is just informal information and should be treated as such.

## What to Look for in a Financial Advisor

You should find a financial professional who has three qualities:

1. Technical competence
2. Independence
3. Strong ethics

If you can locate someone with these three qualities, then you have probably found yourself a good advisor.

## Technical Competence

When assessing technical competence, it is always wise to investigate both the individual's educational background and career experience. Educational backgrounds in finance, tax, accounting, or law are often helpful backgrounds for financial advisors. You should also ask whether the advisor has published any research or papers in the field. Often, advisors who work hard to advance theories in their professions care a great deal about doing a good job and trying to be the best that they can be in their jobs. You can read the advisor's material and get a good sense of his or her philosophy on financial management.

Don't mistake popularity for competence. Remember that finance, like any business, is a lot about sales and marketing. There is nothing wrong with this. Firms need clients to stay in business and grow. They can't provide advice if they don't have a stable client base. But popularity often trumps competence in finance because of the way finance is marketed. It is a personal relationship business, so finance professionals often spend time out in the community on corporate boards and in other high-profile activities. These are all great things to do for the community, but sitting on a board is not much of an indication of competence. It is often more a result of a willingness to contribute to an organization and a result of social networking. It is nice if people do these things, and it is good for the organizations, but it doesn't demonstrate competence in the field of finance. Education, peer-reviewed research, and experience do demonstrate competence, so ask about those things.

For industry experience, you want someone who has had at least 5 to 10 years of working with clients providing financial advice. It generally takes that long to understand how to serve as a good advisor. Knowledge is one thing, but the advisor needs to be able to communicate the knowledge and efficiently service multiple clients at the same time. If you find someone with both strong education and industry experience, they will likely have the skills to make prudent judgments on your behalf.

## Independence

When it comes to independence, you want someone who is working for *you*. Generally, people who work for large brokerage firms or banks have a hard time being independent. There is usually pressure from the big institutions to use products or services that generate the most profit for the firm, as opposed to what is in the best interest of the client. Often, the most independent financial services professionals are those who work for smaller, privately held firms. They are usually on their own because they want to be in a position to give independent advice. Again, this is not always the case, but it is fair to state that you will probably find more independent advisors in privately held firms.

## Ethics

You want an ethical advisor. This means someone who is interested in what is best for you and who makes investment recommendations accordingly. It is important to ask any potential advisors whether they operate under a code of ethics for their firm. Many do and will gladly share it with you. It is also important to find out if an advisor has loyalties to any individual or organization other than his or her clients. If they do, then it may be hard for them to put your best interests first.

You should also check various regulatory databases that collect information about disciplinary actions against financial services professionals. You can access these through the Web sites for the Securities and Exchange Commission (SEC) and the Financial Industry Regulatory Authority (FINRA). Both organizations provide investors with the ability to investigate the backgrounds of brokers and investment advisors. This is additional information to take into consideration. However, just because there are no complaints, that doesn't mean the person is ethical. The opposite is also true. Sometimes there are legitimate disputes between good advisors and clients, and that is just business. We live in a litigious world and people often like to sue if they think they were wronged. That said, it is important to check the official records of anyone you are considering using. Take this information into consideration as part of your overall assessment.

## Finding Your Advisor

Now that you know you are looking for someone who is technically competent, independent, and ethical, how do you find them? Most people find advisors through referrals from other people who they trust. Ask family, professional colleagues, or other professional advisors (such as your accountant or lawyer) if they know of a financial advisor they trust. Then contact any referrals and ask for an initial meeting.

Come prepared with several questions designed to determine if the advisor meets the three criteria we just reviewed: their technical and educational background, their ability to provide independent advice, and their code of ethics. You should also get a clear explanation of how the advisor is paid. Some charge fees, some commissions, and some do a little of both. Both the Securities and Exchange Commission and FINRA also have information on their respective Web sites about selecting an advisor, which is quite helpful.

At the end of the day, a good relationship is one where you have confidence in the person's professional capabilities, their independence, and their ethics, and you think the advisor is a person you will like working with. Remember, you are paying for the advice, so not only should they be good at what they do, they should also be pleasant to deal with.

## Avoiding Fraud

With the collapse in the financial markets over the last year, a number of significant financial frauds have been exposed, the largest to date being the fraud perpetrated by Bernard Madoff. This, of course, has caused many people to wonder what they can do to avoid becoming a victim of fraud. First, it is important to note that the financial services industry is highly secure and safe. Most advisors work very hard to take care of their clients and treat their money with the utmost respect. But, as a consumer, you of course need to understand that there are bad actors in every field, including finance. So what can you do to protect yourself?

Well, you can never prevent all fraud, but there are certain warning signs that should alert you to potential problems. First, be highly suspicious of firms that market great returns. This is how most fraudsters attract clients. They claim to have the ability to earn excessive returns with little to no risk. People like how that sounds, so they are attracted to the marketing. Well, you know from the investment section that to make returns of 10% or more a year, you would need to be fully allocated to stocks, and stocks often decline by a lot. So someone who claims to make lots of money without incurring any risk is probably lying. This is a common technique and generally the foundation of every fraud. Fraudsters prey on people's greed, and they tell them what they want to hear: you can make great returns without any risk. This is not possible.

Second, be suspicious of "secret" investment strategies that the firm won't disclose or that you cannot understand. This is another big, red flag. If an advisor uses a strategy he can't or won't explain, you should be suspicious.

Third, make sure the advisor uses an independent custodian to hold your investments and report to you about what you own. In a number of the recent scandals, the advisor controlled all sides of the investment transaction. He took the money in, decided how to invest it, and then produced the statements that told the clients how much money they had. There was no third-party verification of the accounts.

The vast majority of investment advisors use what is called a *third-party custodian.* These are large financial services firms such as Charles Schwab & Co., Fidelity, and others. The investor opens an account at one of these firms and the advisor manages the money. This creates a critically important separation and level of security. The custodian's job is to process all trades in the accounts and maintain all of your investments. The custodian sends you a monthly brokerage statement that tells you exactly what you own and what it is worth, and they send you confirmations of all trades. If Madoff had used an independent custodian, he would not have been able to tell a client that his account was worth $10 million when the client just received his brokerage statement indicating the account was worth only $1 million. The independent custodian ensures that the client always knows what he or she has and what it is worth. Moreover, most custodians allow clients to view their accounts 24 hours a day via online access.

It is unfortunate that these scandals have done so much damage to investors and to the financial profession's reputation. But fraud is something everyone needs to be aware of and guard against. Be careful about any financial firm or advisor that promotes returns as their primary means of attracting clients, and avoid firms that promise big returns and little risk. This is just not possible. Be sure you understand the fundamentals of how the advisor manages your money. If it doesn't make sense, consider going elsewhere. Be sure the money is kept with an independent custodian so you always get independent verification of what you own, what was done, and what it is worth.

## Alphabet Soup

There are lots of designations in the financial world, and it can be confusing to figure out who is qualified to do what. So I'll take a few minutes to explain two of the main designations that I think are important. Again, you can also visit the Web sites for the SEC and FINRA for more information about these designations. I am not endorsing or recommending one designation over the other. I am simply trying to give you some background to assist you with further investigation and in making the right choice.

- **Registered Investment Advisors.** RIAs are generally registered with the Securities and Exchange Commission or their state securities regulator. A registered investment advisor's primary job is to manage your investments on your behalf, although some also provide advice on retirement planning, taxes, and insurance. The most important thing about an RIA is that the advisor is considered a fiduciary on your account. This is serious business. As a fiduciary, the advisor is charged with being a prudent steward of your funds and must act in your best interest. Essentially, it is their job to oversee and manage your assets on a continuous basis and in accordance with your objectives.

  Registered investment advisors generally charge an advisory fee based on the size of the assets that they are handling for you. It usually ranges from about 1% for accounts under $1 million. What that means is that on a $500,000 investment account, the fee is $5,000 a year. For accounts above $1 million, the fees are generally somewhat less. Some also charge project fees for planning or consulting.

- **Certified Financial Planners.** CFPs are people who have gone through an extensive training and testing program in a broad range of issues that generally covers investments, insurance, retirement planning, and taxes, ultimately becoming certified by the Certified Financial Planner Board of Standards. CFPs also agree to be bound by a code of ethics. The CFP Board is the regulatory body for people who

have the CFP designation. It is a nonprofit organization
dedicated to promoting the ethical and competent delivery
of financial advice. You can visit their Web site at www.cfp
.net for more information.

Certified Financial Planners are often a good choice if you want to
get a financial plan done, want help with your insurance, or want
someone to provide you with recommendations on your investments.
A CFP can also be a registered investment advisor. In that case, he
or she may do both the planning and the investment management
work. CFPs may charge a flat amount to do a financial plan for you,
a percentage of assets that they manage on your behalf, or a commission to buy certain products. Again, it is important to have a clear
understanding of how you are paying for their services. Many CFPs
carry insurance licenses and can help you get insurance coverage.

While there are many other people out there who can provide
you with good help, the only ones I am comfortable suggesting you
consider are Registered Investment Advisors or Certified Financial
Planners, who are subject to a fiduciary standard of care. As a fiduciary, the advisor is required by law to act in your best interest. This
is a very important point and often overlooked. People who agree
to be held to a fiduciary standard are saying something about the
type of work they do and how highly they value their clients. They
are willing to be subject to a higher level of care and responsibility,
which is what you want in a trusted advisor.

Generally, when someone uses an advisor they trust and like, the
relationships can last for many decades. The advisor often knows
more about the family than any other professional service provider.
Because the relationship is so important, spend as much time as you
need investigating your potential advisors, and if something doesn't
feel right, seek a change.

Most good advisors understand that they are not right for every
client. They want to have a good working relationship with the

people they represent, and sometimes a partnership just isn't a good fit. You need a high comfort level on both sides so that advice can be honestly given and you haves clear communication about objectives and goals. In cases where the relationship just isn't working, it is better for both the advisor and the client that they go their separate ways.

## Working with an Advisor

Now that you have located an advisor, how do you work with the advisor and what should you expect? Well, the basis of a good relationship is honesty and trust. The advisor needs to honestly tell you what he or she thinks you should do, and you need to provide the advisor with honest feedback on the advice and how you are feeling. The advisor needs to trust that you will react rationally to his or her advice, and you need to trust that the advice is being given in your best interest. That doesn't mean you will always agree. What it means is that you are both committed to having mature and thoughtful conversations about how to manage your financial life.

It is important to be realistic in your expectations. By now, you should have a pretty good sense that finance is about risk management. Most of the time, you are trying to make decisions in the face of an always uncertain future. Thus, you cannot be guaranteed that things will always work out as you desire, and you have to be realistic about what the financial markets can produce and what your advisor can do for you. Don't expect a miracle worker. Expect someone who helps you prepare for a range of probable outcomes and who helps you make prudent decisions about how to manage your finances. There will be some things that work well and some that don't. That is how it goes in finance. Over the long term, your goal is to do more things that work well than things that don't, and to avoid big mistakes.

You also need to be willing to follow good advice from your

advisor. Many people fail to reach their financial goals because they violate the fundamentals of good risk-management. If your advisor suggests you need to be balanced or more diversified, consider it. Sometimes that means you don't make as much as you thought you could, but it also often means you won't lose as much if things turn against you. The hardest part is executing on the fundamentals when times get good. In bad times, everyone has a heightened sense of risk aversion, and they are often forced by the markets to adjust.

But most of the time the markets are good, and these "up" cycles can run for a long time. This is when people begin to deviate from the fundamentals because they get greedy. If you get greedy, expect that at some point you will pay a severe price. It is very important to consistently execute on the fundamentals; that is what your advisor should help you do. He or she should serve as a check against your greed in the good times and your fear in the bad times.

Finally, because there is no playbook for finance, you and your advisor need to share a common philosophy on financial management and risk. Some advisors are more conservative or more aggressive than others, just as some clients are. There is nothing wrong with either approach; you just need to select one that you think works for you and then find an advisor that reflects your philosophy. It is similar to politics. Some people are Democrats, some Republicans, and some Independents. These are different philosophies that appeal to different people. The same is true with money management.

## Your Advisor's Responsibilities

How should your advisor be treating you? One of the primary things your advisor should do is communicate with you. It is reasonable to expect that you should hear from your advisor several times a year. Sometimes you will have face-to-face meetings, sometimes phone calls, and probably more frequent e-mails.

The assets you hire your advisor to manage will influence the level of service you receive. This is just realistic. Clients with larger accounts that produce more revenue for an advisor should expect and will receive a higher level of service. But because of the advances in technology, a high level of communication can be maintained with clients who may not generate as much revenue. Part of your interview process should be to get a sense of what you can expect in terms of communication and how the advisor likes to communicate with clients in your situation.

Your advisor should also be in a position to stay up-to-date on your personal situation—employment, debt, and so on. Since they are providing guidance, they need to know all about your overall finances and to have a method of keeping track of your information. You should ask about how the advisor does this and what technology and systems he or she uses to support the services provided to clients. A good advisor needs a comprehensive system for efficiently overseeing and monitoring your account. Ask all advisor candidates what systems they use. If they are providing planning and financial models, ask what software they use to create those models and how the models work. These are important issues, because you are paying for guidance and support and you should know the process that helps produce that guidance. Each firm will be different, and you need to understand how your advisor operates.

You should get a clear understanding of your advisor's scope of services. Some advisors focus only on investing. Some provide planning but don't oversee your investments. Planning generally means helping you understand the things we have covered in this book, such as how much you should be saving, how to manage your debt, and insurance. Other advisors do a combination. They manage your investments and provide planning. Depending on your needs, you may want an advisor who does only investing, only planning, or both. Thus, you should clearly understand what your advisor does and then make sure that matches up with your needs.

You also need to understand how your advisor is paid. Some advisors work on a fee-only basis, some on commission, and some on both. Fee-only advisors generally charge a fee based on the size of a client's portfolio, or they charge a flat fee for certain services. As mentioned previously, a common advisory fee is 1% of assets per year for accounts under $1 million, and the fees generally decline for larger accounts. Or a firm may charge a flat retainer of, say, $10,000 a year for certain services. These firms may help you with your investments and other financial decisions, such as insurance or planning, but they only charge fees for their advice.

Other advisors work on commission. The financial services products they recommend have a commission embedded in them. They are paid by the firms that manufacture the product, such as a mutual fund company or insurance company. The client does not directly pay the commission, but in one form or another it is basically incorporated into the fees associated with the product. If there is a commission, ask to have it explained; you need to understand how much your advisor is generating in fees off the products he or she is recommending. Some products may only be available via commission, such as certain insurance contracts. So, you may need to pay commissions on some things, but you need to understand what you are paying and why.

In certain cases, you may be paying a fee to your advisor to manage your assets and then pay him or her a commission if they help you with insurance or other commission-based products. It can be a confusing area, but you should expect that the compensation structure be explained to you. Fees and expenses are a very important issue because the higher the total costs, the tougher it is for you to build capital. There are, however, certain costs of doing business that you should anticipate. Independent and competent advice is not free, so you need to be prepared to pay an advisor fairly for his or her services. In return, the advisor needs to deliver competent, timely, and efficient advice. In general, the lower the fee and investment expenses the better, but bad advice can cost you a lot more than good advice.

The world of investment and financial advice is developing as we speak. It is a relatively new profession, because prior to the last 30 years, not that many people had a lot of wealth to manage. This reflects the fact that our country is a lot richer than it has ever been, and more people have more assets than ever. I expect advisory models to continue to develop over the years as markets and needs change. But today, the primary arrangements are fee, commission, or some combination. Ask a lot of questions and make sure that, at the end of the day, you choose someone whom you feel you can trust in both good markets and bad.

# 14

# Pulling It All Together

At the beginning of this book, I promised you that I would lay out the path from laborer to capitalist. I hope I've done that in a way that was clear and eye-opening. I expect I've given you a lot to think about regarding things like the value of owning a home and the importance of insurance. It's a lot of information, and it could not be more important for your future. So before we part ways, let's spend a few minutes reviewing what you have learned about savings, debt, investments, and insurance, and the overall path you will be taking.

## Your Money Mass Index<sup>SM</sup>

I know I have presented you with a lot of numbers to digest. In finance, it is impossible to get away from numbers. We need the numbers to analyze data and they provide a clear and objective way to assess your financial well-being. The ratios help simplify the math that goes into all of these calculations. You only need to apply a little multiplication and you can get a comprehensive picture of where you should be at each age. But I have taken the simplification even one step further with what I call your Money Mass Index.[SM]

You're probably familiar with the body mass index, which tells you what a healthy weight range is for you based on your height and gender. Well, I created the Money Mass Index to pull together all of the numbers associated with your Capital to Income Ratio, Debt Ratios, savings, and income. The index combines these numbers into one number, at every age, that represents your Money Mass Index. At each age there is also a benchmark Money Mass Index number, and by plugging in your age, income, savings, and debt, I can quickly compare your Money Mass Index to the benchmark. I can then plot, on a nice graph, where you are compared to where you should be.

I invite you to go to my Web site, www.charlesfarrell.com, and run your Money Mass Index. It is easy, and it will show you how far along the path from laborer to capitalist you are. When you get to the Web site, enter the code 778811 and you can get access to the calculator.

I have a Money Mass Index for the three Retirement Income Replacement Rates we have discussed: Age 65 and 80%, Age 65 and 70%, and Age 70 and 70%. When you plot your Money Mass Index, you can clearly see which path you are on. It will also compare your Capital to Income and Debt Ratios to the Benchmark Ratios and tell you how much ahead or behind you might be for your age.

The point of all this is to give you tools that help simplify the process of personal financial management and give you clear direction on the path forward. The simpler and clearer the message, the more likely it is that you can execute on it.

## Luck Is Not a Success Strategy

Now you know what you need to do to progress from laborer to capitalist. The key is to get your savings, debt, investments, and insurance all moving in the right direction. You just need some simple determination to follow the path I have set out for you. To show you how easy it is, I will reduce the entire book to one sentence:

> To go from laborer to capitalist, get a good-paying job, save at least 12% to 15% of pay every year, keep your debt in proportion to your income, invest your money prudently, and get insurance to protect your income and assets.

Best of luck. Of course, if you follow *Your Money Ratios*, you won't need luck, and that's the point of the entire book.

# Special Situations

There are four situations that require individuals to make adjustments to the Savings and Capital to Income Ratios. Let's cover them quickly.

## 1. Traditional Pensions

A traditional pension is a retirement benefit that is guaranteed by your employer. For instance, your employer agrees that if you work for the company for 30 years, your lifetime pension income will be 50% of your pay. These pensions are rare. Only about 10% of employees have a traditional company pension, and that number is likely to shrink over the years. Traditional pensions are costly because they require companies to fund their workers' retirements, and companies simply do not want to take on that expense or liability.

You can look at the financial woes of General Motors as an example of the kind of havoc that taking on too much of the burden of your employee's postemployment period can wreak. Most companies have terminated or frozen their pension plans, and converted to 401(k) plans. But, some people still have traditional pensions, particularly public employees (teachers, police, fire) and some union-based industries.

If you do have a traditional pension, it is going to lighten your requirement to build assets for retirement because your employer is going to do some of the work for you. Thus, you can lower the Savings Ratio and the Capital to Income Ratio by a factor that takes into account your anticipated pension.

If you have a company pension, you need to make an adjustment to what you consider your "income," for purposes of using the Savings and Capital to Income Ratios. The purpose of the ratios is to help you replace your wages in retirement. If your employer has agreed to continue to pay you once you retire, then you don't need to replace 80% of your preretirement income, because you are still being paid by that employer. You only need to replace the percentage of your pay that won't be continued by your employer in retirement.

If your employer agrees to pay you 50% of your wages in retirement, then you only need to replace the other 50% that isn't covered by the pension. Basically, you apply the Savings Ratio and the Capital to Income Ratio to the portion of your pay that will not be covered by your pension in retirement. In this case you would apply the Saving Ratio and the Capital to Income Ratio to 50% of your pay.

Example: Assume we have a 45-year-old worker who earns $60,000 and will have a pension worth 50% of his pay at retirement. This means the worker needs to figure out how to cover the other $30,000 (50% of his salary) with his own retirement savings. Therefore, the worker should benchmark his Savings Ratio and Capital to Income Ratio using the $30,000 of salary he must cover himself. This means his Savings Ratio should be 12% to 15% of $30,000, which is $3,600 to $4,500 a year. At age 45, his Capital to Income Ratio should be 3.7. The Capital to Income Ratio is applied to the $30,000 of his pay that is not covered by his pension. Thus, at age 45, he should have 3.7 times $30,000 saved, or $110,000.

Continuing with another example, assume we have a worker who is 65 years old, was earning $60,000 a year just prior to retirement, and has a pension benefit that was 50% of his final pay. This means his pension is $30,000 a year. If he has been following the Savings and Capital to Income Ratios on the $30,000 of uncovered pay, his Capital to Income Ratio will be 12 at age 65. So multiply $30,000 by 12, and he should have $360,000 in savings. At a 5% distribution, this gives him $18,000 a year of income ($360,000 × 5% = $18,000). Add that to his $30,000 base and he is at $48,000, or 80% of his preretirement income ($48,000/ $60,000 = 80%).

This is why the ratios make planning so easy. They can be applied to any situation. All you have to do is apply a little math to your current situation. Here are the steps for the pension calculation:

1. Determine what percentage of your salary your pension is designed to replace in retirement.
2. Benchmark your Savings and Capital to Income Ratios off the portion of your pay that will not be replaced in retirement.

Pension calculations can be a bit tricky if they are not expressed as a percentage of pay. Some pensions will provide a cash balance amount at your estimated retirement age. Others might apply a dollar amount times years of service, as opposed to a percentage of pay.

Ask your human resources department to provide you with an estimate of your pension benefit based on your anticipated retirement date. They will also be able to provide you with your anticipated salary just prior to retirement. They do this by taking your current salary and making some wage growth assumptions based on inflation. You can then roughly determine what percentage of your final pay will be covered by the pension; then use the uncovered percentage for purposes of the ratios.

While it is great to have a pension benefit, you have to be cautious about the pension estimates. Companies and governments can and do change their pension benefits going forward. If your employer gets into financial difficulty, you may not get as large a pension as you were initially promised. It has been common practice over the last decade for many companies to cut back on their pension programs. They can't reduce the benefits you've already earned, but they can reduce the amount of pension you thought you would earn if you continued to work for the company.

Another situation that can also affect your pension is when a company goes bankrupt. When a company goes bankrupt, the pension assets are safe, but there generally won't be any future contributions to the pension plan. This can leave the plan underfunded, which means the plan may not have enough assets to pay the promised benefits to all of the workers. In this case, you would likely receive a pension, but it will be smaller.

If you are concerned about the stability of your pension benefit and want a little insurance for yourself, boost your 12% to 15% savings rate to cover a larger percentage of your pay. For example, if your pension is supposed to cover 50% of your pay, but you're not sure the funds will all be there in the future, get some breathing room by boosting the savings to 12% to 15% of 70% of your pay. That way, if the pension benefit is reduced, you have your own extra savings to fill the gap. And if it isn't reduced, then you can plan on retiring early. Either way, you win.

You can also boost your desired Capital to Income Ratio by running it against a larger percentage of your pay. In this example, I used 70% of pay. So, take 70% of your pay and apply the Capital to Income Ratio at your age. This figure gives you a goal for your savings accumulation to replace 70% of your pay.

## 2. Sporadically Working Spouse

If one spouse sporadically enters or exits the workforce, this can create some difficulty in estimating your income for purposes of the ratios. I would consider a spouse a sporadic worker if he or she is out of the workforce for five or more years. This can happen for all sorts of reasons. One spouse may stay home to raise the kids or pursue other interests that don't produce wages. In these cases, I suggest you ignore the income of the sporadically working spouse. If this person moves in and out of employment, you cannot count on a consistent cash flow for purposes of determining your Savings Ratio or Mortgage to Income Ratio. If you ignore that income, it forces you to live off the income of the spouse who intends to work for his or her entire career. This will prevent you from overestimating your income and taking on too much debt, or living a lifestyle that you won't be able to support later in life.

When income is available from the sporadically working spouse, you should use those funds to improve both your Savings and Capital to Income Ratios. Save extra during those years and also apply a portion of the wages to paying down your debt. Let's assume one spouse stayed home to raise the kids. Now you are both age 50 and a little behind in your Savings and Capital to Income Ratios. When the second spouse enters the workforce, dedicate a large percentage of that person's wages to increased savings, a higher Capital to Income Ratio, and paying down the debts. The 10 or 15 years of additional wages from this spouse may be enough to get you back on track to retire at age 65, or even help you retire early.

## 3. Age Differences

When using the Savings and Capital to Income Ratios, you need to benchmark your figures based on your age. If there is one primary wage earner in your family, then you benchmark using the age of the primary wage earner.

If both spouses work, then you need to select an age for purposes of benchmarking your family economic unit. Since most spouses or couples are close in age, you simply average their ages. This works for any age gap of less than 5 years. For instance, if you are 45 and your spouse is 41, then you would use 43 as your age.

If, however, both spouses work and you have an age gap greater than 5 years, then you need a two-step process. You average your ages, and run the ratios against the average age. Then, you also should run your separate ratios. You use your own age and income, but split your assets and liabilities in half. The reason you need to do this is because with a large age difference, one of you will likely retire earlier than the other. This means you will have less total household income available for savings and debt reduction.

You likely won't find much of a difference in the numbers if your incomes are relatively close. But if one of you makes significantly more than the other and there is a large age difference between the two of you, then you will have large differences in your ratios. If you fall into this category, you should take the extra steps to get additional insight into your finances.

## 4. Accelerating Income

Perhaps you're one of those fortunate people who experiences a career advance that leads to significant increases in your income later in life. When this occurs, you will need to adjust your Capital to Income

Ratio calculation. The reason is if you have been making $100,000 a year for 20 years, then at age 50 you jump to $200,000, you will find you are way behind in your Capital to Income Ratio once you run it against your new salary. This of course makes sense because you were saving under a much lower income scenario prior to your big raise. What it also tells you is that, even though you received a big raise, you aren't prepared to retire on a lifestyle that replicates that new income.

You need to be careful about the lifestyle decisions you make when you experience a big jump in your salary. Many people automatically ramp up their living expenses to the new salary. They buy a bigger house, more expensive cars, and ratchet up their expenses across the board. And then they still continue to save at the same percentage they were saving before.

The problem is that there is usually not enough time for them to save adequately to hit the Capital to Income Ratio based on their new income. Thus, they may get to retirement and find that they cannot produce 80% of the income from the lifestyle they got used to living for the last 10 to 15 years. This could pose significant problems because they may put too much pressure on their portfolio earnings and run the risk of depleting their assets in retirement.

Example: Assume you are 50 years old, made $100,000, and were on track with your Capital to Income Ratio at 5.2, which means you have $520,000 in savings. Now you get a big promotion and your salary jumps to $200,000. With $520,000 in savings, your new Capital to Income Ratio is 2.6. This means that you are not on track to reproduce 80% of your new salary if you plan on retiring in your mid 60s.

If you continued to save at 15% of your new salary, you would end up with a Capital to Income Ratio of about 8.0, which means you could reproduce about 60% of your new pay in retirement, or about

$120,000. This is much higher than where you were prior to the big raise, but not up to the lifestyle you may be living on the new salary. To get to 12, you would need to save more than 30% of your new salary. The reason is time. There just isn't enough time to build sufficient capital to match a big raise at age 50.

Keep these numbers in mind if you are fortunate enough to see your salary increase substantially later in your career. If you increase your lifestyle, you may be disappointed when you get to retirement because you cannot afford to support that same lifestyle with your savings. The best approach is to split the raise. Take some of it and increase your lifestyle, and then take some of it and increase your savings rate.

Then keep in mind which Capital to Income Ratio path you are on. You may go from the Gold Standard to the Silver Standard based on your new salary. Remember, this will still be much higher than the retirement lifestyle you would have lived on at the lower salary.

# ACKNOWLEDGMENTS

All books are a combination of the efforts of the author plus a lot of other people who helped along the way. I've learned a great deal from many people I have worked with over the years, and would like to thank them for their contributions to my efforts.

First, I have to thank my mom and dad for being such good financial role models, and living these ratios even though they didn't know it. Thanks to Paula, my wife, who had faith in the work I was doing and gave me the appropriate nudge each time I got a little tired and overwhelmed.

I'd like to thank my clients. Each one of you has provided me with great insight into the world of personal finance.

A special thanks to Glenn Ruffenach for graciously reading a very early and rough draft of the book, and for providing me with invaluable insight on the direction and focus of the book.

Thanks to Ted Weinstein, my excellent agent, who agreed to take on the project and kept me focused on my core message. Thanks also to Tim Vandehey, who helped me organize and edit the book, as well as make sure the language was sharp and crisp.

Thanks to Megan Newman and Rachel Holtzman at Avery for their commitment to the book and their guidance through the publishing process.

Thanks to Mark Dorman and Dino Sciulli for helping me understand the workings and importance of insurance.

Thanks to Jonathan Clements, who was an early supporter of my ideas and research in personal finance.

And thanks to Louie, my dog, who sat next to me every day while I was writing this book.

accelerating income, 244–46

activities of daily living (ADLs), 189–90

adjustable-rate loan, 97

Age 65 & 80% Income Replacement (chart), 38–39

aging, costs of, 192

American Dream, 1, 78, 92

animal instincts, 163

art of doing nothing, 163–64

assisted-living facility, 190

auto debt, 108–10

baby boomers, 52, 205

bankrupt company, 242

bear market, 127, 144

Berkshire Hathaway, 164

Big Three automakers, 192

bond market, 115, 147

bonds, 113

   dollar-cost averaging, 152–53

historical return of, 116

intermediate-term, 148, 151–52

municipal, 153–54

in portfolio, 151–55

Treasury Inflation Protected Security, 153

U.S. Treasury, 115–18, 124–25, 132–33, 147–48, 151, 154–55

valuation of, 147

boom-and-bust cycles, 129, 146

borrower, 76

broker, 160

bubbles, 85–86, 128–29, 162

budget, 32–33

Buffett, Warren, 164

bull market, 127, 144

"buy and hold" strategy, 136

"cafeteria plan," 218

calculator, 46

capital, 18

Capital Accumulation Plan (CAP), 32

capitalist, 11–12, 15, 28, 75, 98, 170–71

Capital to Income Ratio (CIR), 15, 58, 82, 88, 117, 120, 125–26
  Bob and Danielle example, 18–19
  calculating, 16–18
  and disability insurance, 134
  80% solution, 19–20
  falling behind, 25–27
  5% rule, 20–23
  how not to run out of money in retirement, 22–25
  and life insurance, 180–82
  situations requiring change to, 27
  special situations, 239–46

career earnings, 101–3

cash value, 184–85

catastrophic disability rider, 175, 177

Certified Financial Planner Board of Standards, 228

Certified Financial Planners (CFPs), 228–29

Charles Schwab & Co., 227

class warfare, 54, 56

coinsurance, 210, 211–12

college fund, 106–8

Commerce Department, U.S., 98

compound earnings, 39–41

computer models, 128

co-payment, 210, 211

costs of aging, 192

credit card debt, 110–11

credit risk, 148

debt
  balancing, 76–77
  credit card, 110–11
  education, 98–108
  healthy, 76
  housing, 77–97
  income-producing, 76
  income-reducing, 76
  Unifying Question, 75

Debt Ratios
  Education Debt to Average Earnings, 99–101
  Mortgage to Income, 79–83

deemed income, 78

demographics, 55

designations, 227–30

disability insurance
  buying, 175–77
  catastrophic disability rider, 175, 177
  group policy, 176–77
  individual policy, 175–77
  maximum benefit, 171
  monthly benefit, 171
  tax-free benefits, 172
  Unifying Question, 170

Disability to Income Ratio, 172–74

discipline, 31

divorce rate (U.S.), 137

doctor bills, 191

dollar-cost averaging, 134–35, 152–53

Dow, Charles, 141
Dow Jones Industrial Average,
        140–41

EAFE index, 143, 149
earnings
    career, 101–3
    compound, 39–41
    history of, 57
education debt, 8, 98–99
    college accountability, 101–3
    rising costs, 103–6
    you come first, 106–8
Education Debt to Average Earnings
        Ratio, 99–101
80% solution, 19–20
emotion, 3
Employee Benefit Research
        Institute, 1
employer contribution, 64–68
excluding Social Security, 58

fear, 163
FICA taxes, 19, 50–51, 191
Fidelity Investments, 227
fiduciary, 229
15-year mortgage, 95
finance, 166
financial advice, 221–22
financial advisor, 222
    avoiding fraud, 225–27
    commission-based, 233
    communication skills of, 231–32
    designations, 227–30
    ethics of, 224–25
    fee-only, 233

finding, 225
    independence of, 223–24
    philosophy of, 231
    scope of services, 232
    technical competence of,
        222–23
financial crisis (2008–2009), 3
Financial Industry Regulatory
        Authority (FINRA),
        224–25
financial media, 165
financial ratios, 5–7
financial services marketing,
        162
five questions, 4–5
5% rule, 20–23
flexible spending account (FSA),
        218–20
foreign investments, 142–43
401(k) plans, 59–61
    contribution limits, 61–63
    employer contribution, 64–68
    IRA rollovers, 60
    Roth, 69–74
    tax savings, 63–64
fraud, avoiding, 225–27
full retirement age, 50
future wages, 101

General Motors, 239
global demand, 144
graduated income tax, 65
graduate school, 100–101
Great Depression, 48, 125, 127,
        133, 135
greed, 163, 226

health-care expense, 191
health-care reform legislation (2010),
207–8, 220
health insurance, 8–9, 207–8
  basics of, 208–12
  coinsurance, 210, 211–12
  co-payment, 210, 211
  deductible, 210, 211–12
  encouraging responsibility,
    213–15
  flexible spending accounts,
    218–20
  health maintenance organizations,
    210
  Health Savings Accounts, 217–18
  High Deductible Health Plan,
    216–17
  how to buy, 215–17
  Human Resources and, 218–20
  indemnity policy, 209
  maximum out-of-pocket cost, 212
  out-of-pocket costs, 215
  preexisting condition, 208
  preferred provider organizations,
    209–10
  premium, 210–11, 215, 216
health maintenance organizations
    (HMOs), 210
Health Savings Accounts (HSAs),
    217–18
health status, 45
High Deductible Health Plan
    (HDHP), 216–17
history, and future, 9–10
home equity, 18
hospital expenses, 191

housing crisis (2008–2009), 81
housing debt, 77–81
  houses are not retirement plans,
    84–86
  income percentage, 81–84
  live where it's affordable, 89–91
  mortgage options, 94–97
  Mortgage to Income Ratio, 79–81
  pay off the house, 87–89
  reverse mortgage, 90–91
  Unifying Question, 77
  when to buy, 92–94
housing prices, 92
Human Resources department,
    218–20, 241

Income Replacement Charts
  Age 65 & 70% of Income,
    41–43
  Age 65 & 80% of Income,
    38–39
  Age 70 & 70% of Income,
    44–45
  Gold, Silver, and Bronze
    Standards, 46–47
income replacement rate, 51
indemnity policy, 209
independent custodian, 226–27
index funds, 148–50
Individual Retirement Accounts
    (IRAs)
  contribution limits, 68
  distribution penalties, 68
  how it works, 69
  rollovers from 401(k)s, 60
  Roth, 69–74

inflation, 22–23
   Savings Ratio and, 35–38
insurance, 8–9
   basics of, 168–70
   disability, 170–74
   health, 8–9, 207–20
   life, 178–87
   long-term care, 188–206
   Unifying Question, 167
insurance agent, 175
interest-only mortgage, 96
intermediate-term bonds,
     148, 151–52
Internal Revenue Code, section
     401(k), 60
investing, 164
investment portfolio, 8
   bonds for, 151–55
   stocks for, 148–51
   volatility and, 126, 131, 143
Investment Ratio
   allocation to stocks and
     bonds, 113–14, 136,
     155–56
   avoiding large losses, 121–24
   long-term thinking,
     133–35
   market return cycle analysis,
     126–30
   offensive and defensive strategies,
     114–17
   Plan B, 132–33, 156
   Plan C, 133
   risk/return trade-off, 117–21,
     136–38, 140
   running the numbers, 124–26

   tips for, 156–58
   Unifying Question, 112
investors, 146
irrational exuberance, 3

laborer, 11–12, 15, 75, 98, 170–71
legacy costs, 192
lender, 76
life expectancy, 52, 118–19
life insurance, 178–80
   buying, 182–83
   need for, 180–82
   permanent insurance, 184–86
   term insurance, 183–84
   Unifying Question, 178
Life Insurance Ratio, 179,
     181, 187
lifestyle, 34, 213–15, 245–46
long-term care insurance
   basics of, 189–90
   benefit pool, 202
   buying, 194–97
   daily benefit, 195
   formulas for care exposure,
     197–200
   inflation adjuster, 195–96
   insurance carrier choice, 206
   only needed coverage, 200–203
   taxation, 201
   term of years, 195
   transition period, 195
   Unifying Question, 188
   waiting period, 196
Long-Term Care Ratio, 203–5
losses, 121–24
luck, 237

Madoff, Bernard, 226–27
market risk, 139
market timing, 3
Medicaid
    asset spend down and,
        193–94
    myths about, 193–94
Medicare, 50, 190–93
    costs of, 192
    Part A, 191
    Part B, 191
    Part D, 191
Money Mass Index, 235–36
mortgage
    adjustable-rate, 97
    15-year, 95
    fixed rate, 94–95
    interest-only, 96
    interest rate on, 95
    negative-amortization, 96–97
    reverse, 90–91
    subprime, 166
    30-year, 94–96
mortgage-backed securities, 162
mortgage debt, 8, 77–81
Mortgage to Income Ratio,
        79–83
municipal bonds, 153–54

negative-amortization loan,
        96–97
Newport, RI, 86
New York Stock Exchange,
        159–60
nursing home, 190

Old-Age, Survivors, and Disability
        Insurance. See Social Security
optimism, 145

past performance, 37
pay as you go, 55
pension calculations, 241
permanent insurance,
        184–86
    cash value in, 184–85
    income level and, 186
    Universal Life, 184
    whole life, 184
personal finance
    four core areas of, 2
    Unifying Theory of Personal
        Finance, 10–12
pessimism, 145–46
Plan B (Investment Ratio), 132–33,
        156
Plan C (Investment Ratio), 133
portfolio, 131
    diversified, 133–35, 138–39
    putting together, 148–51
    risk/return trade-off, 117–21
preferred provider organization
        (PPO), 209–10
premium, 210–11, 215, 216
prepaid death benefit, 185
prescription drugs, 191
pre-spending income, 111
Price to Earning Ratio (P/E Ratio),
        146
primary wage earner, 244
private accounts, 57

professional help, 221
    financial advice, 221–22
    financial advisor, 222
    avoiding fraud, 225–27
    designations, 227–30
    ethics of, 224–25
    finding, 225
    independence in, 223–24
    responsibilities of, 231–34
    technical competence of, 222–23
    working with, 230–31
profits, 31, 143–44
publicly traded company, 140
purchasing power, 36

ratios
    Capital to Income, 15–27
    Disability to Income, 172–74
    Education Debt to Average
        Earnings, 99–101
    Investment, 112–37, 158
    Life Insurance, 179, 181, 187
    Long-Term Care, 203–5
    Mortgage to Income, 79–83
    Savings, 28–47
real estate bubble (2004–2007),
    85–86, 162
real rate of return, 35–38
recessions, 144, 146
Registered Investment Advisors
    (RIAs), 228
renting, 91–92
retirement, 1
    inflation and, 22–23
    money conservation for, 22–25
    at 65 & 70% of income, 41–43
    at 65 & 80% of income, 38–39
    at 70 & 70% of income, 44–45
    Social Security and, 48–58
    where to save your money,
        59–74
Retirement Confidence Survey
    (2009), 1
reverse mortgage, 90–91
risk, 115–17, 129
    changes over time, 131
    credit, 148
    Investment Ratio and, 117–21
    market, 139
    putting in perspective, 136–37
    specific, 139
    U.S. Treasury bonds and, 148
Roaring 20s, 127
Roosevelt, Franklin Delano, 48
Roth vs. Traditional plans, 69–74
Russell 3000, 142, 148–49

savings, 7–8, 28
    401(k) plans, 59–68
    Individual Retirement Accounts,
        68–69
    Roth vs. Traditional plans, 69–74
    taxable investment account, 74
savings rate, 84
Savings Ratio, 58, 82
    calculating, 29–31
    cutting spending, 34
    habit of saving, 35
    Income Replacement Charts,
        38–39
    inflation and, 35–38
    living on a budget, 32–33

Savings Ratio *(cont.)*
     profit and discipline in, 31
     retiring at 65 & 70% of income,
          41–43
     retiring at 70 & 70% of income,
          44–45
     secret of two times pay, 39–41
     special situations, 239–46
Securities and Exchange Commission
          (SEC), 224–25, 228
self-employed retirement
          accounts, 61
slippage, 33
Social Security, 21–22, 48–49, 177
     change and, 52–53
     essentials of, 53–56
     excluding benefits, 58
     how it works, 49–52
     paying fair share for, 56–58
Social Security Disability Insurance
          (SSDI), 177
Social Security Trust Fund report
          (2009), 53
special situations
     accelerating income, 244–46
     sporadically working spouse, 243
     spousal age gaps, 244
     traditional pensions, 239–43
specific risk, 139
spending, 34
spouse
     age gaps, 244
     sporadically working, 243
spread, 37
Standard & Poor's 500, 115, 138,
          140–42, 148–49

stock exchanges, 140
stock market, 115
     components of, 140–43
     declines in, 116
     return cycle analysis of,
          126–31
stocks, 113
     historical return of, 115–16
     profits and, 143–44
     valuation of, 144–46
     volatility in, 126, 131,
          143, 156
subprime mortgages, 166

taxable investment account, 74
tax-deferred accounts, 64, 68
taxes
     disability insurance, 172
     FICA, 19, 50–51, 191
     flexible spending accounts,
          218–20
     401(k) plans, 63–64
     Health Savings Accounts, 217–18
     long-term care benefits, 201
     municipal bonds, 153–54
term insurance, 183–84
third-party custodian,
          226–27
30-year mortgage, 94–96
traditional pensions,
          239–43
Traditional plans, 69
Treasury Department, 55
Treasury Inflation Protected
          Security (U.S. Treasury
          bond), 153

underwriting, 175
Unifying Question, 12–13
  credit card debt, 110
  Debt Ratios, 75
  disability insurance, 170
  education debt, 98
  housing debt, 77
  insurance, 167
  Investment Ratio, 112
  life insurance, 178
  long-term care insurance, 188
Unifying Theory of Personal
    Finance, 10–12
Universal Life insurance, 184
U.S. Treasury bonds, 115–18,
    124–25, 132–33, 147–48,
    151, 154–55

vesting schedule, 66
volatility, 126, 131, 143, 156

wage base, 50
wage growth/housing cost
    relationship, 85
Wall Street, 121
  as euphemism, 160–61
  gimmicks of, 161–63
  ignoring, 159
*Wall Street Journal, The,*
    141
wasting assets, 109
wealth transfer, 54, 56
whole life insurance, 184
World War I, 127
World War II, 35

Charles J. Farrell, J.D., LL.M., is a principal with Northstar Investment Advisors, an investment management firm in Denver. He writes the "Retirement Roadmap" column for the CBS MoneyWatch site and contributes a monthly retirement column for advisers to *InvestmentNews*. His research is frequently cited in *The Wall Street Journal*, *SmartMoney*, the *Chicago Tribune*, and many other consumer and professional media outlets. He lives in Denver.